Confronting
Abusive
Beliefs

Interpersonal Violence: The Practice Series
Jon R. Conte, Series Editor

Interpersonal Violence: The Practice Series is devoted to mental health, social service, and allied professionals who confront daily the problem of interpersonal violence. It is hoped that the knowledge, professional experience, and high standards of practice offered by the authors of these volumes may lead to the end of interpersonal violence.

In this series...

Confronting
Abusive
Beliefs

Group Treatment
for Abusive Men

Mary Nõmme Russell
with Jobst Frohberg

Interpersonal Violence:
The Practice Series

SAGE Publications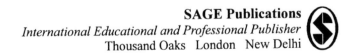
International Educational and Professional Publisher
Thousand Oaks   London   New Delhi

For information address:

SAGE Publications, Inc.
2455 Teller Road
Thousand Oaks, California 91320
E-mail: order@sagepub.com

SAGE Publications Ltd.
6 Bonhill Street
London EC2A 4PU
United Kingdom

SAGE Publications India Pvt. Ltd.
M-32 Market
Greater Kailash I
New Delhi 110 048 India

Printed in the United States of America

Library of Congress Cataloging-in-Publication Data

Russell, Mary Nõmme.
    Confronting abusive beliefs: Group treatment for abusive men / Mary Nõmme Russell with Jobst Frohberg.
        p. cm. — (Interpersonal violence : the practice series; v. 12)
    Includes bibliographical references and index.
    ISBN 0-8039-5807-2 (alk. paper). — ISBN 0-8039-5808-0 (pbk.: alk. paper)
    1. Abusive men—Counseling of. 2. Group psychotherapy. 3. Abusive men—Psychology. 4. Wife abuse—Prevention. I. Frohberg, Jobst. II. Title. III. Series: Interpersonal violence; v. 12.
RC569.5.F3R87 1995
616.85'8220651'081—dc20   95-21329

This book is printed on acid-free paper.

95 96 97 98 99 10 9 8 7 6 5 4 3 2 1

Sage Production Editor: Tricia K. Bennett

Contents

PART IV: GROUP SESSION PROTOCOLS

PART V: PROGRAM OUTCOMES

Preface

This book was written primarily as a guide for therapists working with abusive men. It has particular relevance for therapists who are interested in exploring novel approaches and new theoretical foundations for their work. In presenting an alternate theoretical framework and detailed group session protocols, the book provides sufficient background and detail for inexperienced therapists and students yet also provides a novel and different perspective for experienced practitioners in this field.

The book also has relevance for the study of the gendered nature of relationships. Relationships in which men abuse their partners are a relatively common phenomenon, and the present in-depth study of abusive men's belief systems provides a perspective that up to now has been lacking. To what extent such belief systems are shared with nonabusive men was not determined, but the present findings provide a starting place for further study.

Therapists, students, and academics with an interest in the theory and practice of group psychotherapy can benefit from the innovations presented. The application of interactional psychotherapy principles to treatment of wife abuse provides a unique perspective. The process and effect of mixed gender group leadership has been extensively considered. Using the group process as a medium of belief confrontation represents an extension of both groupwork practices and belief systems theory.

Views of individuals with different perspectives were systematically considered and integrated in the process of developing the present model. Therapists working with assaulted women as well as those working with assaultive men were involved in discussions of the various aspects of evolving treatment. Abusive men participating in the program provided continual feedback regarding the relevance of the group to their lives. Partners of these men were also asked to provide feedback regarding their perceptions of the men's progress.

Theoretical perspectives that were integrated included those pertaining to belief systems, interactional group therapy, male violence, male socialization, and the gendered nature of relationships. Belief systems theory that had previously been applied only to individual change was extended to encompass group therapy with abusive men. Theory related to male socialization and male abusiveness was incorporated in the process of defining the problem. Theory pertaining to the gendered nature of relationships was used in defining treatment goals. Integration of diverse but complementary theoretical perspectives has resulted in a unique foundation for this treatment approach.

The *Confronting Abusive Beliefs* model is one that evolved as repeated clinical applications, monitoring through standardized measures, and follow-up of group completers and their partners provided feedback regarding effectiveness of program elements. Clinical applications indicated that some group practices increased individual resistance to rather than promoted change, and, as a result, these were deleted or modified. Standardized measures indicated that some psychological changes, such as level of emotional expressiveness, were uncorrelated with abusive behaviors, so such topics were reconceptualized. Feedback from group completers indicated that elements of the process, such as group interactions, were particularly helpful, so these were emphasized. Feedback from partners indicated that instruction in cognitive-behavioral modifications alone tended to be counterproductive, so psychoeducational methods were de-emphasized and belief confrontation was developed as the primary group intervention.

Confronting Abusive Beliefs, although primarily a book about group therapy with assaultive men, is also about theory and research. The advances in theoretical development, the production of empirical data, and the integration with and application of these in the development of a practice model can be considered the signal contribution of this work.

Acknowledgments

This book represents the contributions of many people and organizations. Family Services of Greater Vancouver was the setting in which this program was piloted and evaluated. Therapists associated with the Family Violence Program were actively involved in implementing and refining the program as well as confronting and modifying the conceptual framework and beliefs on which it is founded. Nick Phillips, as Program Coordinator, facilitated the implementation of the program. Gail Zuk and Jill Corey, as leaders of women's groups, were instrumental in confronting and challenging the many beliefs about men's treatment groups that impede movement toward respectful relationship beliefs. Mark Rayter and Chris de Boer, as fellow men's group leaders, were helpful in using their experiences to assist in the articulation of the present program components. Without the participation and engagement of this devoted and supportive team of therapists, this book would not have been possible.

Participation of the many men in the program and research was essential to the success of the project. The men not only voluntarily

sought treatment for their abusiveness but also willingly participated in completing measures and interviews. The men's voices
articulating their beliefs and describing their efforts to move toward
respectful beliefs provided profound insights. Likewise, their partners participated in providing alternate perspectives on the relationships through their completed measures and their comments.

Finally, the Family Violence Prevention Division, Health Canada,
provided the necessary funding for the development and evaluation
of this program. David Allen provided vital assistance and support
in bringing the project to completion.

Connection with the lives of many diverse individuals has been
an invaluable aspect of this work, and I hope all have been enriched
through this process of mutual engagement.

PART I

Introduction

1

Shifting Paradigms in the Treatment of Abusive Men

Understanding of and explanations for men's abusiveness toward their female partners have undergone extensive transformation over the past decades. From believing that such behavior was normal and inevitable, society has moved to viewing such behavior as criminal, pathological, and unacceptable. From believing that a man's abusive behavior toward his spouse was a private matter, current social norms view abusive behaviors as requiring social interventions of a criminal and/or therapeutic nature. From explaining male abusiveness as infrequent social deviance, current knowledge has revealed it to be commonplace and pervasive.

This altered understanding of abusive male behavior has required a corresponding shift in social and therapeutic remedies. Criminal sanctions have been applied, and although acknowledged as necessary, they alone have not been sufficient (Dutton, 1988). Behavioral therapies based on notions of male deficits have been applied and have been found to be of limited effectiveness (Gondolf, 1986). To bring about comprehensive and enduring change in men's abusive behaviors, a treatment model that extended beyond punitive and behavioral interventions was necessary.

Confronting Abusive Beliefs represents a *paradigm shift* in therapeutic interventions from the prevailing male deficit model to a belief systems model. It shifts the emphasis in treatment from negative sanctions and behavioral reinforcements to the belief systems that support and sustain men's abusive behaviors. Belief systems change is deemed necessary to alter the behaviors commonly displayed by abusive men to respectful interactions with their female partners.

Changing beliefs requires an understanding of the complex nature of belief systems, an understanding of the multifaceted nature of beliefs, and an understanding of the confrontational process required to produce change. Each of these topics is addressed in subsequent sections of this book. The aim is to provide therapists working with abusive men a different perspective on abuse and to describe how this perspective translates into a successful therapeutic intervention.

❏ Influence of Social
Beliefs on Treatment Models

The commonly held belief that men's abuse of women is normal, humorous, or inevitable is increasingly being challenged. Men are finding that behavior that previously may have been acceptable or desirable evidence of masculinity now meets with negative social responses and sanctions. Jokes about woman abuse are more likely to be regarded as deviant or embarrassing than funny. Reports of physical abuse by women are likely to result in police actions such as removal of the man from the home, incarceration, and criminal charges (Edleson & Tolman, 1992). Community surveys report an overwhelmingly negative response to questions about the acceptability of physical and psychological spousal abuse (Sigler, 1989).

One result of this change in social beliefs is that abusive men increasingly seek to alter such behaviors and participate in treatment programs. Some do this voluntarily, others are "wife mandated" or attend at their wives' insistence, whereas others do so in response to court orders. Men are beginning to understand that abusive behaviors are incompatible with respectful intimate relationships.

Treatment programs of various types have been developed in response to this increased demand (Feazell, Mayers, & Deschner, 1984; Pirog-Good & Stets-Kealy, 1985). The most common type of program has been group treatment with a behavioral focus. These programs have aimed to reduce physical violence through behavioral methods such as "time out," relaxation, behavioral monitoring, and assertiveness training (Roberts, 1984). Some programs have supplemented this behavioral focus by including discussions of sex role attitudes with the view to modifying stereotypic male attitudes considered to be associated with violent behavior (Dutton, 1988; Edleson & Tolman, 1992; Pence & Paymar, 1993). Feminist approaches that specifically focus on men's negative attitudes and devaluation of women have also been developed (Adams, 1989; Almeida & Bograd, 1991).

The underlying assumption in all these programs has been that of a *male deficit*. Abusive men, it is assumed, are deficient in ways of controlling anger, of expressing their wants assertively and their emotions appropriately, or of sufficiently and positively valuing women. These deficit assumptions, however, do not explain why some of the so-called deficits are situation specific, others are not necessarily associated with abuse, and traditional sex role attitudes alone are not sufficient to explain the pervasiveness and persistence of men's partner abuse.

The supposed deficiency in controlling anger for many men is largely restricted to their female partners in the privacy of their own homes. In other situations and with other persons, these men are quite able to control their anger. Assertiveness and emotional expressiveness may well be lacking in some abusive men, but there is no evidence that increasing levels of these skills reduce abuse or that expressive and assertive men are not abusive. Attitudinally, although abusive men typically denigrate their partners, they have not been found to hold significantly more traditional attitudes toward women than nonabusive men (Hotaling & Sugarman, 1986), nor does instruction alone result in cessation of abuse. Deficit explanations, therefore, are demonstrably incomplete in explaining men's abuse of female partners. Treatment programs based on these models, therefore, are likely to be limited in effectiveness.

Empirical evaluations of behavioral programs based on deficit models indicate that outcomes, although generally positive, tend to be short term and limited to reductions in physical abuse. Programs focusing on male deficits have been found to be generally successful in reducing violence levels of men who attend, but have been less successful in long-term maintenance of nonviolent behavior or in decreasing psychological and other types of abuse (Saunders, 1989; Tolman & Bennett, 1990). In fact, studies have indicated that some programs that result in decreased physical abuse have little effect on or may even increase psychological abuse (Gondolf, 1986; Tolman & Bhosley, 1991).

To produce enduring and comprehensive change from abuse to respect in relationships requires a theoretical perspective and treatment model that addresses fundamental aspects of self and relationships. A theoretical perspective that provides an understanding of abusive men's belief systems regarding themselves and their relationships is necessary. A treatment model that focuses on and attempts to modify these beliefs could be expected to produce more substantial change.

❑ Belief Systems That Support Abuse

Belief systems theory provides the framework for a comprehensive and fundamental understanding of self and relationships. Belief systems theory posits that the organization of personality rests on the basis of individual beliefs that direct behavior and influence affect and cognitions (Ball-Rokeach, Rokeach, & Grube, 1984; Rokeach, 1979). Abusive behaviors, therefore, can be conceptualized as reflecting basic beliefs about the self and the other in relationships. These beliefs both direct and support abusive behaviors as well as mediating the affective and cognitive processes that accompany abuse.

Belief systems change has been advocated as one that produces more enduring and comprehensive alterations in attitudes and behaviors (Rokeach, 1985; Rokeach & Regan, 1980). Beliefs, as individual expressions of basic values, are considered to have a greater effect on behavior than behavioral reward and punishment. Beliefs, as a basic element of personality, influence a range of behaviors and are influential in directing much of social interactions. Beliefs are complex entities that integrate emotional, cognitive, and behavioral aspects. To change abusive behaviors, therefore, a method that confronts beliefs that support such behavior is necessary.

> *Abusive belief systems are characterized by beliefs in the centrality, superiority, and deservedness of the self.*

BELIEF SYSTEMS OF ABUSIVE MEN

Belief systems of abusive men studied as part of the development of the present program were found to be characterized by beliefs in the *centrality, superiority,* and *deservedness of the self.* These beliefs were found to be linked with a potential for abusiveness. An abusive man's belief in the centrality and separateness of the self precludes a definition of his behavior as abusive by disregarding effects of this behavior on his partner. His belief in the superiority of the self permits him to devalue his partner well as to justify abusiveness as a necessary defense to his threatened superiority. An abusive man's belief in deservedness of the self provides justification for abuse when his needs are not met.

These abusive beliefs are contrary to beliefs in connectedness, equality, and mutuality that are necessary for respectful relationships. The aim of the program, therefore, is to foster change from an abusive belief system to a respectful belief system as presented in Table 1.1.

Belief systems change is necessary to eliminate the range of abusive behaviors that are displayed by abusive men in their relationships. The *Confronting Abusive Beliefs* program provides a means of focusing on belief systems and promoting this change process. To understand the desired outcomes in this program, a definition of abuse is necessary.

Table 1.1 Abusive and Respectful Relationship Beliefs

Abusive Beliefs	Respectful Beliefs
Self as central and separate	Self as connected
Self as superior	Self as equal
Self as deserving	Self as mutually engaged

❏ Definitions of Abuse and Respect

Because this program aims to decrease the entire range of abusive behaviors, an encompassing definition of abuse was required. Physical violence was subsumed under the general category of abuse, which was considered to also include psychological, economic, and sexual abuse.

The definition of abuse used in this program was as follows:

> Abusive behavior is behavior that inflicts hurt or injury through disregard, domination, or inequitable demands of the partner. Abusive behaviors include use of physical violence, demeaning language, domination, and demands for service.

This definition is based on the premise that abuse occurs within an interpersonal and social context characterized by gender inequality (Murphy & Cascardi, 1993). A belief in the superiority and dominance of the male in a relationship provides the context for abusive behaviors. Abuse in such contexts connotes excessive or exploitative expressions of power by men over their female partners.

Abuse is not necessarily motivated by a man's will to hurt, as suggested by Kuypers (1992), but can result from his simple disregard or lack of consideration of consequences of actions on his partner. Abusive men's beliefs in their centrality and deservedness provide a context that can support abuse.

Abuse is ultimately defined by the consequences of the behavior as determined by the experience of the female partner. The power to determine whether a particular behavior was abusive is assigned to the man's partner and is based on her experience as the recipient of particular actions. The elimination of abuse requires that the female partner no longer feels abused.

In contrast to abusive behaviors, respectful behaviors were considered those that were conducive to the development of mutually satisfying relationships. Such relationships have been extensively studied at the Stone Center, Wellesley College, and the present definition reflects the resultant formulations of Jordan, Kaplan, Miller, Striver, and Surrey (1991).

The definition of respectful behavior used in this program is as follows:

> Respectful behavior is behavior that conveys consideration for the partner as an equally valued person and connects with her in a mutually engaged fashion.

This definition posits beliefs and behaviors based on connectedness, equality, and mutual engagement. As such, it diminishes the likelihood of abusiveness. When a man believes his partner to be equal and engages with her in a mutual and connected fashion, the resultant interaction conveys respect. Respectful relationships promote the development of intimacy and inhibit abusive tendencies.

❑ Changing Beliefs to Produce Behavior Change

Belief systems theory postulates that behaviors are directed by beliefs and that cognitions and affect are mediated by beliefs.

Changing behaviors, cognitions, or affect requires a change in beliefs. Men's belief systems that support abusive behaviors, therefore, become an appropriate target for change.

Abusive behaviors are incompatible with respectful intimate relationships.

Belief systems theory takes into account the cultural and social contexts that sustain beliefs and deter belief change. Abusive men's beliefs are developed and sustained in a social context that reinforces male centrality and domination of women. Belief systems change necessitates the development of a therapeutic context in which prevailing norms of masculinity can be confronted and alternates explored.

Changing belief systems can be conceptualized as the primary goal of psychotherapeutic processes. Psychotherapy has been described as a social interaction that aims to change the client's belief system to be more congruent with that of the therapist (Rokeach & Regan, 1980). This convergence has been demonstrated to be one of the outcomes of successful therapy (Beutler & Bergan, 1991).

Belief change involves more than simple cognitive change, and therefore, psychoeducational approaches alone are insufficient. Changing beliefs involves affective involvement and self-evaluation within an interpersonal context. Group processes in which beliefs are confronted provides a milieu that fosters such change.

The process of belief change involves several steps. Because beliefs may exist below conscious awareness, the first step is one of articulating the belief and bringing it to awareness. This is followed by highlighting the dissatisfaction with or the difficulties caused by the present belief system in order to increase motivation to change. The present beliefs are then confronted and contrasted with alternate beliefs. These alternate beliefs are shown to be more conducive to the establishment of a respectful relationship.

This change is facilitated when beliefs are confronted in a group setting. A group provides multiple sources of input and reinforcement. A group setting for abusive men also provides an environment that permits breaking taboos associated with stereotypic masculine beliefs. Groups also tend to develop a sense of collectivity in struggling with the development of new beliefs. Men's development of an altered belief system about themselves in relationships appears to be particularly fostered in groups that include a female co-leader.

The process of belief change, the theory underlying it, and the nature of group therapy with assaultive men are the subject matter of this book.

❏ **Outline of the Book**

This book is organized to provide a comprehensive guide to the theory and practice of the *Confronting Abusive Beliefs* program. Part I provides an introduction and overview to the book. Part II describes the theoretical background related to belief systems in providing an overview of belief systems theory, describing the process of changing beliefs, outlining the belief systems of abusive men, and contrasting this with a respectful belief system. Part III describes the theory and practice of group treatment by discussing the group as a medium of change as well as presenting the practicalities of group formation and structure.

In Part IV, the group session protocols for implementing the program are provided. The primary tasks of each phase of the group process such as setting the stage, confronting abusive beliefs, developing respectful beliefs, and consolidating changed beliefs are described. Part V presents an overview of program outcomes, including results of standardized tests as well as intensive, follow-up interviews with group participants. Handouts for distribution throughout the program are reproduced in the Appendix. An overview of belief systems theory and a description of the belief systems of abusive men, accompanied by the discussion of the process of belief change and detailed session-by-session group therapy protocols, have been provided as guides to therapists wishing to implement this program. Used in a sensitive and flexible manner, this approach has been found to result in significant reductions in both physical and psychological abuse among men who complete the program.

PART II

Theoretical Background

2

The Influence of Beliefs on Behavior

Changing an abusive man's orientation toward his female partner requires a fundamental and profound alteration in his view of himself, his partner, and the relationship. Belief systems theory provides a framework for understanding how beliefs as basic aspects of a man's worldview influence his interpersonal functioning. Furthermore, this theory proposes the manner in which fundamental beliefs can be altered to produce comprehensive and sustained change.

Belief systems theory posits that individual cognitive, affective, and behavioral processes are regulated by beliefs, attitudes, and values. Values and beliefs that are most fundamental to the personality have the most pronounced and enduring effect on behavior. Change in these fundamental beliefs is likely to produce the most comprehensive behavioral change.

Beliefs regarding the self and relationships are central to the way in which intimate relationships are structured. The beliefs of abusive men, therefore, provide the support and direction for their abusive behaviors. Understanding the nature of these beliefs is necessary to consider how change can be brought about.

❏ Origins and Development of Belief Systems Theory

Belief systems theory is based on the study of values, most comprehensively explicated in the work of Milton Rokeach (1967, 1979, 1985), further developed by Robin Williams (1979) and Lynn Kahle (1983, 1984), and most recently extended by Sandra Ball-Rokeach, Milton Rokeach, and Joel Grube (1984).

A variety of definitions of basic terms such as beliefs, values, and attitudes have been used in developing this theory. Distinctions in terminology, although not necessarily critical in a therapeutic context, provide clarity in theoretical presentations. Definitions for terms as used in the present discussion are therefore provided below.

❏ Definitions of Values, Beliefs, and Attitudes

The following definitions are based on those presented by Rokeach and Regan (1989) and Ball-Rokeach et al. (1984).

Values. Values are abstract, global, and socially shared ideals of behavior and end-states of existence. Values are few in number in that they are broad and encompassing and include concepts such as "freedom," "happiness," "peace," and "equality." Values consist of higher-level abstractions or organizations of more specific beliefs.

Beliefs. Beliefs are more specific and concrete individual expectancies concerning existence, evaluation, prescription-proscription, or cause. Beliefs, or the individualistic reflections of values, regulate individual actions in specific situations or conditions. Beliefs are more readily articulated by individuals than values and, therefore, can be more readily identified and confronted in therapy.

Attitudes. Attitudes refer to evaluative beliefs that have direction. Attitudes can be subsumed under the concept of beliefs.

Thoughts. Although thoughts typically refer to cognitive processes, individuals frequently express aspects of their beliefs as thoughts. For example, an abusive man may recount, "As I listened to her, the *thought* that she shouldn't be criticizing me kept running through my mind."

Because of their common usage and more direct and concrete aspect, beliefs and thoughts can be usefully discussed in the therapeutic context. Beliefs, however, are not limited to cognitions, as they also mediate affective responses and direct behaviors. Questions about men's thoughts, therefore, can be used to elicit aspects of fundamental beliefs. Discussions of beliefs and thoughts can be productive, whereas discussions of values and attitudes tend to become abstract and impersonal and be of limited benefit.

❏ Dimensions of Beliefs and Their Connection With Abuse

Belief systems are complex entities that affect behaviors and social interactions in a variety of ways. Knowledge about the ways that beliefs can support abusiveness is useful both in raising awareness of beliefs and in fostering belief change. In the following discussion, the term values is used synonymously with beliefs, reflecting the earlier literature that did not distinguish between them.

BELIEFS HAVE EXPLICIT AND IMPLICIT DIMENSIONS

Belief systems exist along a continuum of explicitness ranging from the inchoate, unconscious, and suppressed to the articulated, conscious, and expansive. Unconscious beliefs can be inferred from a person's behaviors or statements. Williams (1979) describes these differences as follows:

> Some values are indeed highly explicit and appear to the social actor as phenomenal entities: The person can state the values, illustrate their application in making judgments, identify boundaries and the like. Other standards of desirability are not explicit and social actors may even resist in making them explicit. Nonetheless, some criteria of this kind can be inferred from selective behavior, and when such inference is presented to the behaving actor some individuals can recognize in their own conduct a value of which they had not previously been aware. (p. 17)

Because many beliefs regarding social interaction between men and women are embedded in the social fabric, these beliefs are frequently accepted without conscious awareness or examination. Men who derive benefit from these socially accepted beliefs benefit further from a lack of examination and lack of protest about these benefits. Abusive men, for example, who expect subservience and servility from their female partners may do so without awareness of the belief system that underlies their expectations. They also may be reluctant to examine the belief system that benefits them.

BELIEFS HAVE COGNITIVE, AFFECTIVE, AND DIRECTIONAL ASPECTS

Individuals' statements about beliefs provide information not only about their thoughts but also about their feelings and the likely direction of their actions. Although beliefs may be experienced as thoughts or cognitions, they also serve to mediate emotional responses and to direct behaviors. For example, an abusive man who states his belief that he deserves his partner's undivided care and attention on returning home from work is describing not only his thinking but his emotional predisposition as well as his likely behavior toward her. If his partner instead presents him with complaints, arguments, or concerns of her own, he may feel quite justified in responding abusively.

BELIEFS HAVE EVALUATIVE
OR JUDGMENTAL ASPECTS

Beliefs incorporate standards that generally have been developed socially. Rokeach (1979) states:

> [They] are standards that are to a large extent derived, learned, and internalized from society and its institutions. . . . They serve as standards or criteria to guide not only action but also judgment, choice, attitude, evaluation, argument, exhortation, rationalization and . . . attribution of causality. (p. 2)

Thus, beliefs are the bases on which evaluations are formed, on which judgments about what is "right" are made. Abusive men frequently assume that the judgments they make are based on unassailable, rational criteria that their partners should respect. Challenges to the "rightness" of their judgments, even about minor disputes, can trigger abusive behaviors.

BELIEFS HAVE CULTURAL, RELATIONAL,
AND INDIVIDUAL COMPONENTS

Beliefs are developed in and derived from a cultural context, they are used to direct or structure social relations, and they influence and are influenced by psychological processes.

Williams (1979) states, "In the enormously complex universe of value phenomena, values are simultaneously components of psychological processes, of social interactions, and cultural patterning and storage" (p. 17).

Understanding this tripartite aspect of belief systems is important when developing ways and means of modifying abusive belief systems.

The *cultural component* denotes that beliefs are learned in a process of ongoing, continuous adaptation to the prevailing social context. Rokeach (1973) theorizes that "the antecedents of human values can be traced to culture, society, and its institutions" (p. 3). Klugel and Smith (1986) describe the pervasive influence of socialization on developing individual beliefs, particularly those related to maintaining inequalities and devaluing other social groups. Because male socialization begins early, is sufficiently consistent, and is reinforced by diverse societal influences, the beliefs developed are difficult for an individual to realize, let alone overcome. Beliefs regarding male centrality, superiority, and deservedness are of this nature.

Influence of and identification with a social reference group is an important element in maintaining belief systems, particularly when beliefs define other groups to be lesser or inferior. In such cases, beliefs of the superior group prevail and subjugation of others becomes acceptable. Abusive men subscribing to the dominant belief in male superiority frequently justify abusiveness as a necessary means of suppressing perceived threats to their superiority by female partners. This need to "show her that the man is boss" is a cultural prescription that can lead to abuse.

Similarly, beliefs regarding the appropriate expression of emotion by men are cultural prescriptions that mediate the display of affective reactions. For example, fear is inconsistent with a belief in male superiority and, therefore, is more likely to be expressed as anger. Anger is not only consistent with the stereotype of male superiority but also can be instrumental in reinforcing that superiority, frequently in an abusive fashion.

Understanding the cultural and social context of beliefs leads to an appreciation of both the possibilities of and difficulties in producing change. Because socialization into a belief system is a learning process, relearning also can occur. However, because socializing influences are so pervasive and ubiquitous, the countering influences that promote resocialization must also be profound.

In times of rapid social change, such as the present, the possibility of procuring change is likely to be heightened. For example, a man who was reared in a family in which wife abuse was acceptable is at risk of repeating such behavior with his partner (Hotaling & Sugarman, 1986). However, his partner may have been influenced by emerging feminist beliefs that condemn such abuse, and she may invoke personal as well as social sanctions should such abuse occur. Cultural prescriptions during times of social change are less likely to be consistent, increasing the possibility of change.

The *relational component* denotes that values are an inextricable part of social relations, including intimate male-female relations. Kahle (1983) states that "relations are primarily exchanges of values, and values dictate relations. . . . Values only emerge from social interactions" (p. 276). This suggests that men's abuse of women is supported and dictated by their beliefs about themselves and their place in relationships.

Abusive men are characterized by beliefs that support dominance and separateness.

Williams (1979) describes dimensions of beliefs in social relations as including equality versus inequality, autonomy versus dependence, and submission versus dominance. Abusive men are characterized by beliefs that support dominance and separateness. These beliefs make abusive behaviors possible.

Behavior in intimate relations, therefore, is directed by the beliefs held about the place of the self in relation to the other in such relationships. Furthermore, men's behavior provides an indication of relationship beliefs. For example, a man who regularly fails to listen or attend to his partner is likely to be acting on the belief that her communications are of no importance to him. His behavior conveys the disrespectful beliefs he holds, thus decreasing the probability of developing a respectful and satisfying relationship.

The *individual or psychological component* of beliefs is linked with self-esteem as beliefs serve as the "conceptual tools and weapons" used to maintain and enhance self-esteem (Rokeach, 1973). Abusive men's beliefs, therefore, can be used to rationalize and defend behaviors in an effort to preserve their superior status and maintain the associated heightened self-esteem.

Klugel and Smith (1986) suggest that the psychological process of cognitive mastery, including a sense of control, is used to maintain an individual's belief system. Abusive men's behavior can frequently be seen as an attempt to maintain mastery or control, particularly when their belief that they should dominate women is threatened.

Klugel and Smith further suggest that evidence of consistency and congruency of beliefs is conducive to satisfaction, whereas evidence of inconsistency or lack of congruence can lead to dissatisfaction and change. Dissatisfaction of this nature is central in the process of altering belief systems of abusive men. For example, an abusive man's belief in the centrality of the self in a relationship may permit him to ignore the effect of his abusive behavior and retain his perception of himself as nonabusive. However, when confronted with evidence of the effects of his behavior, as well as his partner's and society's definition of his behavior as abusive, the likelihood of dissatisfaction and propensity for change is increased.

BELIEFS GUIDE BEHAVIORAL CHOICES

In social interaction, continuous choices are being made about how to act, what to say, and so on. Williams (1979) states that beliefs provide the "complex precodings of behavioral choices" (p. 21). From the range of possible behaviors in a specific situation, one's belief system directs or limits the choices that are made.

Abusive men frequently lack awareness of behavioral choices.

Abusive men frequently lack awareness of behavioral choices they make and of the influence of their beliefs on these choices. They may be quite adamant that their abusive behavior is *not* a choice. For example, many abusive men describe their abuse as an "automatic" or "spontaneous" reaction—one over which they had no control. Or alternately, they describe their abusive behavior as being externally generated. For example, "she pushed my buttons" is a frequent explanation for abusive behavior that denies the possibility of choice. Demonstrating to abusive men that their behavior always reflects a choice and increasing their awareness of the benefits of alternate choices are therefore necessary to promote change.

BELIEFS ARE BOTH FORWARD AND BACKWARD LOOKING

Williams (1979) describes beliefs as guiding goal-directed behavior as well as justifying past conduct. For example, an abusive man's belief in male superiority may lead him to choose to physically restrain his partner. He may later justify this behavior by explaining that his partner had been "unreasonable," and thus his use of restraint was justified in the situation. Both the behavior and the justification arise from the belief in male superiority.

❏ Summary

Understanding the nature of belief systems provides insights into the forces directing, maintaining, and justifying the behaviors of abusive men as well as providing direction for therapeutic change efforts. Understanding that beliefs may exist below conscious awareness; that they can support judgments of an absolute nature; that they have emotional as well as cognitive components; and that they are shaped by cultural, social, and psychological influences provides a context and direction for a treatment program for abusive men.

3

Changing Abusive
Men's Beliefs

Psychotherapy can be considered a process aimed at altering clients'
belief systems. The impetus to seek change can come from negative
consequences such as legal sanctions or partner responses in the case
of wife abuse. Dissatisfaction with such consequences can motivate
men to consider therapeutic options. In the course of group therapy,
abusive men who believe in inequality and superiority in intimate
relationships, and use abusive behaviors to enforce these beliefs, are
confronted with the negative consequences of these beliefs. The process of group interactions demonstrates the positive outcomes associated with the contrasting beliefs in relationship mutuality, connectedness, and equality. The therapeutic process fosters
examination, confrontation, and modification of abusive beliefs
and adoption of the latter beliefs that promote mutually satisfying
relationships.

To bring about change in existing belief systems, it is necessary to
bring these beliefs to awareness, to emphasize dissatisfaction with

existing beliefs, and to provide models of alternate beliefs. Group therapy with abusive men that changes abusive beliefs to respectful beliefs can be expected to produce a comprehensive and enduring decrease in abusiveness.

❑ Group Therapy as a Belief Change Process

Psychotherapy has been described as a social interaction that consists of expression of beliefs between client and therapist, with the goal of resolving the client's problem through alteration in the client's belief system. Rokeach and Regan (1980) described this as "value therapy," and London (1964) described it as a "moral exchange." In work with abusive men, the moral aspect of denouncing abusive behavior is explicit, as evidenced in a shared goal of working toward elimination of abuse.

Therapy outcome is said to be dependent on the joint influences of the beliefs of the client and the therapist and the social context within which the process is embedded (Rokeach & Regan, 1980). Positive outcome has been defined as movement in the client's values toward those of the therapist to produce "value convergence." Increased similarity between client and therapist values following successful therapeutic interventions has been noted (Beutler & Bergan, 1991; Rosenthal, 1955). In group psychotherapy, client beliefs become the focus of change, alternate beliefs are articulated and modeled by group leaders, and beliefs prevalent in the social context may support or impede belief systems change.

The aim of group therapy with abusive men includes the explicit goal of eliminating men's abusive behavior. Changing the abusive belief systems that support the abuse is an effective way of reaching this goal. The focus of the group interaction, therefore, is the confrontation of men's abusive beliefs with the aim of replacing them with respectful beliefs.

Therapists' personal beliefs have a significant effect on the change process because they determine the direction of change.

Therapists must themselves believe in equality, mutuality, and connectedness in intimate relationships if they aim to promote client change in this direction. These therapists need to develop strategies for monitoring the beliefs they convey to ensure that these are not inconsistent with their espoused therapeutic goals. One such strategy is regular consultation with women's group representatives, feminist therapists, or women leading battered women's groups.

Influences in men's social context must be considered in changing abusive belief systems. Given the pervasiveness of abusive beliefs and a therapeutic goal of fostering beliefs that run counter to prevailing ideology, the lack of supportive influences for respectful beliefs needs to be addressed. Therapeutic groups for abusive men provide a nonthreatening setting in which beliefs that run counter to prevailing beliefs about men in relationships can be expressed and explored. Therapists need to encourage group members to develop additional supports for these beliefs outside the group. Having such support will reinforce the development and maintenance of respectful beliefs.

Consideration of client beliefs, therapist beliefs, and the social context supporting beliefs requires a multifocused perspective in belief change therapy. Each of these aspects must be kept in mind throughout the process of belief change.

❏ Steps in Producing Belief Change

Beliefs exist on a continua of conscious awareness or "mindfulness" (Langer, 1989). The process of bringing about belief change, then, requires bringing the relevant beliefs to awareness, heightening the dissatisfaction with current beliefs, altering old beliefs, and promoting and strengthening new beliefs. In group therapy with abusive men, the beliefs that are brought to awareness are those that support abusive behavior, and the ones that are promoted and strengthened are beliefs conducive to respectful relationships with women.

BRINGING BELIEFS TO AWARENESS

Beliefs that direct behavior in intimate relationships are largely absorbed from the social context without a high degree of conscious awareness. Sex role socialization begins in infancy and continues through the life span, providing reinforcement for beliefs considered gender appropriate and negative sanctions for those that are not. Because socialization influences are constant and pervasive, the process of acquiring the beliefs tends to be unnoticed. The beliefs adopted are rarely subject to scrutiny. Beliefs such as male domination in intimate relationships, including the use of abusive behavior to maintain such domination, have until recently been accepted unquestioningly. Negative valuation of women then becomes virtually reflexive as men believe women's deference and submission to be the norm.

When men's beliefs about themselves, their partners, and their relationships support abusive behavior, the first therapeutic task is to bring these beliefs to awareness. Because beliefs are conveyed both in words and in actions, awareness can be heightened by focusing on the language men use as well as their behavior.

Language used by abusive men frequently provides an indication of their beliefs about their relationships. For example, abusive men's language often conveys the belief that they are not responsible for their abusiveness. Phrases such as "something snapped," "it just happened," or "it got ugly" indicate that the man believed his abusive behaviors were outside his control. Alternately, a belief that the partner was culpable is evidenced in statements such as "she pushed my buttons," "she should have known better," or "she shouldn't have provoked me." Bringing these beliefs regarding the responsibility for abusiveness to awareness is essential if abusive behavior is to be changed.

Language regarding the relationship between the self and the partner also provides indicators of abusive beliefs. When a partner's complaints are dismissed as "PMS" or her financial management is derided as "throwing money down the toilet," an abusive man conveys his belief in male superiority and his partner's inferiority in the relationship.

Behaviors convey beliefs, sometimes in concordance with and at other times in opposition to stated beliefs. Some abusive men, for example, will explicitly state their belief in male superiority, whereas others proffer a belief in relationship equality but at the same time dominate their partners. Individual behavior, therefore, requires scrutiny to determine what beliefs are being conveyed so that these, as well as any inconsistencies between the conveyed and stated beliefs, can be brought to awareness.

AUGMENTING DISSATISFACTION WITH CURRENT BELIEFS

Belief systems, even when examined, can be stable and resistant to change. Motivation to change usually derives from dissatisfaction or distress that is either internally or externally generated. Augmenting such dissatisfaction is useful in increasing motivation to change.

Self-dissatisfaction, or an internally derived "noxious affective state," has been described as an impetus for change by Rokeach (1973). Self-dissatisfaction stems from observed discrepancies between one's self-ideal and one's actual behaviors, or between what one says and what one does. An individual temporarily can resolve such discrepancies by using various psychological processes such as rationalization, projection, and denial. However, more enduring, comprehensive, and ultimately satisfying change is brought about by change in the belief system.

Abusive men frequently expend considerable energy engaging in various psychological defense mechanisms such as denial, minimization, and justification. However, although these defensive processes temporarily may assuage guilt, they rarely produce increased self-satisfaction. Furthermore, typical outcomes of men's defensiveness are increased psychological distance and mistrust between the man and his partner.

External influences also can increase dissatisfaction with belief systems. When there is a discrepancy between beliefs and desired external outcomes, dissatisfaction or distress is likely to ensue. An abusive man's dissatisfaction can be increased through his partner's refusal to accept abuse, through the partner's taking steps to leave the relationship, or through the partner's retaliation. Social sanctions such as police intervention and arrest are additional external influences that increase dissatisfaction and motivation to change.

Motivation to change beliefs, therefore, can be increased when psychological influences as well as external forces converge to augment dissatisfaction. The impetus for change is greatest when dissatisfaction is derived from multiple sources and the abusive beliefs are consistently confronted and challenged.

CONFRONTING BELIEFS

Dissatisfaction with current beliefs provides the possibility for change, but changing beliefs also requires self-evaluation and adoption of new beliefs. Both emotional and cognitive processes must be engaged for change to take place. Confrontation of beliefs and belief change can be promoted in interpersonal exchanges as part of therapeutic group process.

Keeping abuse secret permits the abusive behavior to continue.

Self-evaluation is a process whereby each man considers whether his behaviors are consistent with his ideals, whether his stated beliefs are consistent with his behaviors, and whether his beliefs direct behaviors that have desired consequences. When discrepancies are confronted, particularly those that might require relinquishment of advantage derived from male supremacy, defensive reactions are likely to be engendered. Rokeach (1973) suggested that self-evaluation should be a private process because this would decrease defensiveness. However, when confronting beliefs sustaining male abusive behavior, a private process can be dangerous. Keeping abuse private allows men to avoid negative social consequences that result from more public disclosures. Abusive men's belief that they are not responsible for the consequences of their actions is not challenged when the abuse is kept secret. Keeping abuse secret permits the abusive behavior to continue.

Belief change for abusive men can involve extensive self-evaluation. This process of evaluating and confronting beliefs frequently is reported by abusive men to result in considerable confusion and distress. For example, men report that they begin to question all their beliefs and values, they no longer have faith in many of the guiding principles in their lives, and decision making often becomes difficult. As men evaluate beliefs that previously had directed their lives and find them wanting, the articulation and modeling of alternative beliefs can provide direction in resolving this confusion.

Adoption of new beliefs is promoted by articulation and modeling of such beliefs. Research on persuasion has indicated that messages delivered by credible models will result in belief change (DeBono & Harnish, 1988; Petty & Cacioppo, 1986). Group leaders and other group members who articulate and model respectful relations can provide examples of alternative beliefs as well as the benefits to be derived from those alternative beliefs.

New beliefs also can be fostered through providing different interpretations for observed behaviors. For example, a man's disclosure of fear can be redefined from an indication of weakness to an act of courage. A man who is struggling to cope with his own sadness or dejection rather than projecting blame and anger onto his partner can be defined as displaying strength and fortitude. A man who listens to his partner and acknowledges the validity of her perspective can be redefined from being submissive or a "wimp" to being respectful and mature in his actions. Behavior that has been labeled negatively as unmasculine or as an indication of weakness can in such a manner be redefined as strength or courage that contributes to respectful relations.

Because the steps of bringing belief to awareness, augmenting dissatisfaction with present beliefs, confronting beliefs, and adopting alternate beliefs rely largely on verbal interactions, group leaders require facility in use of various therapeutic methods of this nature. The following section describes some of the therapeutic methods that can be used.

❏ Methods of Producing Belief Change

QUESTIONING

Bringing beliefs to awareness or increasing dissatisfaction with beliefs can often be accomplished most appropriately through simple questions. Questioning men about the justification that preceded or accompanied their abusive acts can yield information about their abusive beliefs. Simple questions such as the following can be used:

What was going through your mind as your partner was refusing to go along with your plans?

What was the first thought that came into your mind as your partner criticized you for spending all that money?

Can you explain what you mean when you say that you expect your partner to "respect" you?

REFLECTION

The group process provides a rich source of interactions that group leaders can reflect on. The reflections can relate to present interchanges within the group, or to previous ones reported by group members. The female and male co-leaders can use their particular gendered perspectives as part of these reflections.

The female leader can reflect the ways in which particular actions or exchanges affect her as a woman. For example, reflections on present group interactions can include the following:

I notice that when I ask you a question, you direct your responses to the male group leader rather than to me.

The male leader can use his gender, for example, to reflect on a group member's difficulty in disclosing personal failings:

I notice that it's hard for you, as it often is for me, to admit that you hadn't considered the effect of that act on your partner.

CHALLENGING QUESTIONS

One of the most powerful methods of confronting beliefs and/or encouraging consideration of alternate beliefs is the posing of challenging questions. Challenging questions can be defined as those that not only aim to bring beliefs to awareness but also raise questions regarding the consequences of the present belief or alternate belief. This kind of questioning, which was developed as part of *values clarification* methodology, focuses on the alternatives, consequences, and actions associated with different beliefs (Glaser & Kirschenbaum, 1980; Raths, Harmin, & Simon, 1966). In the context of abusive men, therefore, these questions attempt to elicit beliefs by emphasizing the consequences of present abusive beliefs or alternate respectful beliefs. Examples of challenging questions include the following:

> When you get angry because your partner disagrees with you, does that mean you believe she doesn't have the right to disagree with you?
>
> When you blame your partner for your abusiveness, what does that say about your belief about being responsible for your own actions?
>
> When you call your partner a "bitch," what does that say about the way you regard her?
>
> You say that you want your partner to "respect" you but your actions indicate that you expect her to *obey* you. Do you believe that obedience is the same as respect?

Challenging questions, by counterposing beliefs and actions or beliefs and consequences, therefore, effectively confront the group member with his beliefs. They also can be used to promote consideration of alternate beliefs as follows:

> If the most important consideration for you was the effect your actions had on your partner, how do you think your behavior would be different?
>
> If you were to acknowledge that your partner works hard looking after the children and the home, would you still be able to call her "a lazy slob"?

Less effective challenging questions are those that are too general or address social rather than personal issues. These questions tend to elicit intellectual debates rather than self-evaluation. For example, even though it is probable that abusive men's beliefs regarding their partners are linked with low regard for women generally, addressing the latter, for the most part, fails to result in productive responses. An example of a challenging question of this nature to be avoided is the following:

> When you use such negative language to describe your partner, what does that indicate about the way you think about women?

The response to questions such as this is typically a denial of sexist attitudes and rebuttal that because men are increasingly accused of subjugating women, they are the real present-day victims.

Similarly, challenging questions tend to be less effective when they are not congruent with objectives of the particular group phase. For example, in early group sessions, simple questions that aim to bring beliefs to awareness are more productive than complex challenging questions that address consequences or alternatives. Similarly, toward the end of the program, simple questions directed toward alternative beliefs are most effective in promoting the integration of alternatives. Challenging questions that counterpose beliefs and consequences or alternatives generally are most productive during the middle phases of the program when the aim is to increase dissatisfaction with present beliefs and encourage the exploration of alternatives.

❏ Summary

The argument that psychotherapy is essentially a process of belief change has received considerable empirical support. Bringing about such belief change involves a number of steps. These include bringing beliefs to awareness, augmenting dissatisfaction with existing beliefs, confronting beliefs, and developing alternate beliefs. Challenging questions, when timely and personally directed, can be powerful instruments in achieving these outcomes. Abusive men, when made aware of and confronted with their abusive beliefs, can be engaged in the process of belief and behavior change.

4

Confronting Beliefs
of Abusive Men

Abusive men's belief systems, conceptualized as complex integrations of affect, cognitions, and behaviors, have not previously been subject to systematic and intensive study. Furthermore, studies of abusive men's characteristics have not provided much data in this regard. The present investigation was conducted to determine to what extent and in what ways belief systems of abusive men were linked with their abusive behaviors.

Results of previous studies were reviewed to determine to what extent the findings about abusive men's characteristics could be interpreted in the context of a belief systems analysis. In addition, previous findings were reviewed in terms of their adequacy in explaining abuse and providing direction in therapy with abusive men.

❏ Characteristics of Abusive Men

Several empirical investigations of abusive men's characteristics have included belief systems indicators, but these studies have yielded contradictory results. For example, abusive men have been found to be excessive adherents to male sex role stereotypes (Caesar, 1985; Telch & Lindquist, 1984), deficient adherents to sex role stereotypes (Rosenbaum, 1986), and no different from nonabusive men in their adherence to such stereotypes (Rosenbaum & O'Leary, 1981). Although there is an indication that some connection between sex role stereotypes and abusive behavior might exist, the nature of the relationship is not clear.

Similarly, studies of assertiveness or use of power have reported confounding results. Abusive men have been found to be lacking in assertiveness (Maiuro, Cahn, & Vitaliano, 1986), excessively needing power (Dutton & Strachan, 1987), and no different from nonabusive men in authoritarianism (Neidig, Friedman, & Collins, 1984). Again, although abusive men's use of power is commonly considered by therapists to be a factor in abusiveness, the studies reported have not been able to clarify the relationship between these variables.

Hotaling and Sugarman (1986, 1990) in two separate research reviews of abusive men's characteristics concluded that the characteristics most strongly associated with male abusiveness relate to their social environments rather than particular characteristics of the men. Their findings indicate that exposure to violence in families of origin and high levels of marital conflict are the factors most consistently and most powerfully associated with male abuse. They conclude that the problem experienced by abusive men is a lack of opportunity to learn appropriate conflict resolution skills. The assumption they make is that abusive men fail to learn such skills because of the inherently violent nature in which they are raised. The appropriate remedy, they suggest, is to provide abusive men with skill training in conflict resolution.

In contrast to the suggested conflict resolution skill deficiency, clinical observations have indicated that many abusive men are highly proficient in conflict resolution. The problem, therefore, is not a lack of skills, but rather the choice of situations and contexts in which to use such skills. A belief systems interpretation suggests that abusive men, influenced by personal, familial, and social factors, have developed a belief system condoning marital violence as a way of resolving or avoiding conflict. Belief systems theory further suggests that neither teaching behavioral skills nor providing information about alternate attitudes is adequate in bringing about belief change. A process that engages men in becoming aware of, evaluating, and confronting beliefs is necessary.

To determine the extent to which abusive men's belief systems supported their abusive behavioral choice, an investigation of these belief systems was deemed necessary.

❑ A Study of Abusive Men's Beliefs

Abusive men's beliefs about their place and nature of participation in intimate relationships with female partners previously has not been studied. As part of the present work with abusive men, 15 abusive men participated in intensive interviews that aimed to describe their belief systems in relation to themselves and their place in intimate relationships. The men were interviewed following program completion. The period of follow-up ranged from 3 to 18 months.

The interviews invited the men to reflect on beliefs they held prior to entering the program, to describe ways in which their beliefs changed during the program, and to articulate their present beliefs as well as perceptions of further changes necessary. Although the accounts of initial beliefs were retrospective, they were generally supported by specific examples providing validation of these accounts. Interviews ranged in length from 30 minutes to 1 hour. All interviews were recorded and transcribed.

Analysis of interview transcripts was based on Strauss and Corbin's (1990) grounded theory methodology. The analysis yielded common themes that represented men's beliefs about themselves and the ways in which these were used to justify abuse. Because of this observed link with abusiveness, these beliefs have been labeled *abusive relationship beliefs.*

Table 4.1 Abusive Beliefs and Their Consequences

Abusive Belief	Consequence
Self as central and separate	Disregard of partner Disregard of consequences of own behavior
Self as superior	Partner regarded as inferior Domination of partner Abuse justified to sustain dominance
Self as deserving	Caring as one-way interaction Abuse justified when expectation of care not met

❑ Abusive Relationship Beliefs

Men's beliefs about their place in relationships guide their inter-actions with their partners. Beliefs that place the man in a central position that disregards the partner's welfare, beliefs that place the man in a superior position and support actions to preserve this superiority, and beliefs that place the man in a position of deserved-ness that justifies actions to enforce his expectations can all be termed abusive beliefs in that they can lead to abusive actions.

In the present study of abusive men's beliefs, there was a striking concern for the self as central with a concomitant absence of consid-eration of the partner. There was a conviction that abusive behaviors were necessary to maintain the man's superiority and dominance, frequently accompanied by a fear that loss of such control would result in the man's subjugation by the partner. There was a common perception that the man's home and intimate relationship existed primarily to restore and comfort the man as he returned from his forays into a hostile outside environment. Failure of partners to meet such expectations were considered deserving of coercive actions.

These beliefs together formed the core of abusive men's under-standing of intimate relationships. These beliefs, furthermore, served to promote, sustain, and justify abusive actions. These beliefs and their consequences are summarized in Table 4.1.

Treatment of abusive men requires understanding of their beliefs, the manner in which they are expressed, and the ways in which they support abuse. The following discussion presents each belief and typical statements made by men that illustrate that belief.

THE CENTRAL SELF

The *central self* is the primary theme in the belief systems of abusive men. Contrary to suggestions that abusive men have negative or hostile beliefs about women, the present analysis indicated a virtual absence of consideration of women, or at best fleeting thoughts that were quickly suppressed.

Ignoring or not attending to the effects of their behavior on their partners permitted the men to maintain their beliefs in their own essential goodness or nonabusiveness. When evidence such as physical or psychological trauma was routinely disregarded or dismissed, the abusive men had no reason to evaluate their own actions or beliefs. As long as they were able to sustain such disregard, the men had no difficulty in perceiving themselves as unhappy, wronged souls who had simply reached their breaking point.

The abusive men's beliefs about women were not as much negative as they were absent.

The abusive men's beliefs about women were not as much negative as they were absent. When their partners asserted themselves and demanded that they be taken into account, this was frequently perceived as threatening and resulted in an escalation of men's abusive actions.

The belief in the central self reflects an extension of the masculine ideal of autonomy and individuality. Autonomy, in the extreme, precludes consideration of others. Lack of consideration of others, in turn, permits guilt-free enactment of abusive behaviors, because exclusive focus on the state of the self results in ignoring observed effects of abuse. Abusive men, therefore, considered themselves as troubled or wronged *but nonabusive* because they chose to ignore the consequences of their actions on their partners. The central self, therefore, is also defined as a nonabusive self because partners are largely disregarded.

The Central Self as Nonabusive

Abusive men were able to define themselves as nonabusive by focusing exclusively on their own states of being and ignoring consequences of their actions. Because they did not consider the effect their behaviors had on their partners, they were able to maintain that they were nonabusive. As the men were describing their abusive behavior, they frequently made comments, such as the following, that illustrate their lack of awareness of the consequences to their partners:

> I wasn't abusive, only angry and unhappy.
>
> Since there wasn't a pattern or nothing, I didn't think it [the abuse] was a major problem.
>
> I didn't think I was abusive because I didn't have any sense of the scope of a basic relationship.
>
> I thought violent guys were the scum of the earth, real deadheads, beating up on women, [whereas] I had only pushed . . . never really beaten my wife.

The common element in these statements is the absence of any consideration of the partner or the effect of the behavior on the partner. The men described their actions *only and exclusively* from their own perspective, from their view in the center. Their inability to perceive their behavior as abusive was genuine, as their view was limited to their own perspectives: They were unhappy, they only did it once, they didn't fit the stereotype of a batterer. Their beliefs about relationships did not include consideration of the effects of their behavior on their partners. When the behavior is viewed only from the perspective of the self, it then becomes a simple matter to deny abusiveness. The belief that the other is inconsequential allows men to avoid applying the label *abusive* to their own behavior.

When consequences of the men's behavior on their partners intruded into the exclusivity of the central self, the abusive men had little difficulty in disregarding the intrusion. For example, when partners refused to silently suffer the effects of abuse, the men's statements displayed a consistent belief that these effects or consequences were unimportant, transitory, or not worthy of attention.

The statements indicate a belief that by defining these events as unimportant, the consequences could be avoided.

Sample statements that defined consequences as unimportant include the following:

> I didn't fully think it [my behavior] was OK, but I didn't give it much thought.
>
> The consequences of my anger . . . I guess I just put them out of my head.
>
> [My behavior] with my wife . . . I just thought, well, it doesn't matter, whatever I did would blow over in a day or so.

It was important for the abusive man to minimize the partner's concerns and in this way remain separate and disconnected from her. Only by ignoring or dismissing the effects of their behavior on their partners could they maintain their self-definition as nonabusive.

The belief in the central self included justifying actions aimed at maintaining the self in a distress-free state. The partner's actions were routinely evaluated in terms of their effects on the central self, and frequently implicated when distress was experienced.

The partner's behaviors frequently were described as causing distress and as such were justifiably subject to retaliation. Abusive behavior toward the partner then became a justifiable course of action, a way of indicating that causing distress to the self was unacceptable and to be avoided at all costs. Abuse was justified, partners were blamed, and the self was absolved. Examples of such self-justifying and partner-blaming statements include the following:

> I was unhappy with all the stuff my wife was doing. . . . When I got pissed off I became abusive, *according to her*, but I figured she deserved it, pushing my buttons like that.
>
> I was always trying to put the blame on her, make her the goat. . . . I kept saying to her, "Well, why didn't you do this?" you know, basically blaming her.
>
> A lot of blame was aimed at her for not knowing that she should handle me more carefully, and respond more appropriately when I'm under a lot of stress.

The common belief evidenced in these statements is that responsibility for maintaining the abusive man's central self in a distress-free state resides with his female partner. It follows, then, that if the man feels distressed, the responsibility resides with his partner, and abuse toward her is justified. Not only are the men absolved of responsibility for their abusive behavior, but any constructive or remedial action becomes the partner's responsibility. Further justification of abuse is provided by the belief that partners as inferiors should be compliant.

THE SUPERIOR SELF

The belief in the *superior self*, with the man being dominant in an inherently hierarchical relationship, was one of the fundamental aspects of abusive men's belief systems. Competitiveness, an intrinsic part of male socialization, is reflected in abusive relationships in the assumption that positions in the relationship are defined by who is greater and lesser. For abusive men, retaining dominance and superiority were essential in their relationships with their intimate partners. Challenges to dominance by partners were viewed as insurrections requiring coercive action.

> *Challenges to dominance by partners were viewed as insurrections.*

The self as superior, expressed in domination of the female partner, was such a pervasive belief that it generally was regarded as not requiring articulation. The abusive men in the present study, with the advantage of self-evaluation and hindsight, were able to express the beliefs that had directed their abusive behaviors as follows:

> You're my wife, you should trust my opinion. The twist in this is that you don't necessarily need to have your own [opinions].
>
> I would make the decisions and go around and she didn't seem to have a problem with that. . . . [I believed] that the man was head of the household and the final decisions should be his. You know, there has to be a boss. I would make the decisions, my word was the last word. My word was law.
>
> I'd put my own ideas in my wife's head. I always thought if I did this . . . then she should do that.

The firmly entrenched belief was that the man's opinions, decisions, and ideas should dominate. The partner, without question, should accept these and acquiesce. The possibility that the partner might have her own perspective was disregarded, and any effort on her part to differ with the superior male made her subject to abuse.

Paradoxically, the men who resisted defining themselves as abusive, nevertheless were able to recognize the instrumentality of violent or abusive behavior in maintaining their superiority and authority. Although these insights were derived from men following completion of treatment, the way in which they describe their violence suggests that even as they were being violent they were mindful of their goal of achieving their partners' subjugation. Abusive men's statements regarding their use of violence to subdue their partners include the following:

> If I didn't get what I wanted, I would get violent because things were not going my way.
>
> I guess I believed that if I can get away with treating her like shit, then, what the hell! I mean, why not? . . . I'm always right and even if I'm not you'd better not say anything or you are going to pay the price.
>
> When I just didn't want to argue any more or I didn't want to discuss the problem, I got violent, and that was basically the end of it.
>
> The violence stopped my partner from doing things I didn't like.

These statements reveal an awareness of socially and physically derived male superiority that has utility in maintaining a man's control over his female partner. Furthermore, none of the men expressed any reticence in using this superior status, indicating a belief that it is their inherent right to do so.

The belief in the superior self rests on an assumption that all relationships are hierarchical in nature. Male socialization reinforces notions of hierarchical relationships in emphasizing the need to be competitive to attain status and to be vigilant to threats against such status. However, in any system based on inequality there is a continual possibility and threat of rebellion by those who have been subjugated. Attempts by the female partner to alter the relationship are viewed as evidence of insurrection rather than attempts to establish equality. Her actions, therefore, must be quelled because, in the man's view, his partner's success in rebellion would result in her domination over him. This fear of insurrection and reversal of the hierarchy from male domination to female domination was evident in the present study. The men articulated this belief as follows:

> I had a siege mentality and somehow I figured that if I didn't act first then she would get me.
>
> I always have been the one to make decisions and I felt that if I didn't I would feel put down.

This either-or notion of dominance in relationships precluded any consideration of equal input, shared activity, or mutual involvement. For some abusive men, competition for dominance was paramount and subjugation by the partner was to be avoided at all costs. Abusive behavior frequently was exercised and justified in this context.

THE DESERVING SELF

The belief in the *deserving self* was characterized by men's demands to be cared for and have their needs given priority. The men had no awareness that a relationship entailed a mutual process that involved consideration of needs of both parties. Caring, nurturing, supporting, and giving were believed to be one-way processes: from the partner to the man. Care and attention were due to the man because of his more important and stressful role. The partner's caring for children or family frequently was viewed as a detraction from the attention due to the man. Partners who failed to provide the requisite care and attention to the man were considered to deserve abuse.

Abusive men believed that their partners should provide appreciation, comfort, and solace to counter the harsh everyday world in which they functioned daily. They invariably described their interactions with other men in the course of their work as hostile, unwelcoming, and threatening. In contrast, they believed that their homes should be sanctuaries, places to which they could retire, be comforted, be nurtured, and be restored so that they could again venture out into their hostile male worlds.

The men's relationships with other men were uniformly described in negative terms:

With other men, it's like you're competing with them, or against them, or fighting them.

I felt like everyone was shitting, dumping, and ragging on me for things that I had no control over . . . like my money and my laziness.

In contrast, the men believed that their family relationships should be different, centered on appreciating the efforts of and restoring the beleaguered male:

I always felt that at home I was safe, that this was my safety place, that nobody here was going to be mean to me or disrespectful or yell at me. I always thought when I was home I was safe and I could tell my wife about whatever problems I had.

I thought that [my partner] should appreciate what I, the man, as king of his castle did for her.

This notion of sanctuary provides no consideration of the partner as a separate person with experiences or needs of her own. When the realities of the home, in the sense of the experiences of the partner and/or children, intruded, the men believed this to be a violation, a situation in which they could legitimately be angry and abusive:

I felt that a kind of sanctuary had been taken away from me and I resented that and that made me mad too . . . my last sanctuary on earth where I could feel safe and that had been taken away from me by my wife and kids.

I'd get mad at work and then somebody wouldn't be doing what I told them at home, and I'd say "Jesus Christ! It's the same thing at home as it is at work."

Here I am . . . trying to get ahead. My wife didn't appreciate it. She was always bitching and complaining. . . . I had just gotten shit from my boss for screwing up on an order and he had the nerve to tell me to smarten up. I had come home in a pissed-off mood and, anyway, then my wife started getting on my case again. I got so mad I grabbed a knife.

A corollary of looking to the partner for comfort and solace is a lack of ability to nurture or care for the self and a dependency on others to provide such care. The men were only able to begin verbalizing this lack within themselves, which led to their dependence on their partners. One man was able to express it as a mutual dependency:

> We've always been very close and in some ways sort of dependent on each other.

Another man, who had changed considerably while in the group, expressed his concern about having switched his dependency from his wife to the group:

> What's going to happen when the group's finished? I mean, I'm not going to have anyone to talk to . . . I hope I can talk to my partner. . . . I don't want to be dependent on the group or have someone else solve my problems.

The men expressed little confidence that they could adequately care for themselves. Furthermore, there was no conceptualization of a relationship in which partners were mutually engaged in caring for each other.

An important corollary of the belief in deservedness was its extension to deserving forgiveness and forgetting of past abuses. Abusive men frequently indicated that because they had acknowledged their abusiveness and felt that they had dealt with it, it should no longer influence their partners' behavior toward them. There was no understanding or appreciation that past abuse provided a context for their partners' present experience, that partners may continue to be fearful and mistrustful for a considerable length of time, and that partners needed to deal with relationship issues according to their own timetable, not one dictated by the man. The following is an example of a statement indicating this type of deservedness:

> About 3 months before we split up, I said, look, we either go and get some help now and deal with the problem that we have together or this relationship is going to end.

Many abusive men indicated that by participating in group treatment they had absolved themselves of blame. The only problem that still existed was that their partners could not forget about the abuse.

They felt resentful that they had not been forgiven for the abuse when this was what they clearly deserved.

❏ Summary

Beliefs in centrality, superiority, and deservedness of self expressed by abusive men not only permitted them to choose abusive behaviors but also presented barriers to development of respectful relations.

As long as abusive men are unable to directly confront the effects or consequences of their actions on their partners, as long as they do not treat their partners' reactions as important, as long as they disregard their partners' fear and pain, it is unlikely that significant change can ensue. As long as they believe that relationships are inherently hierarchical and unidirectional, that they need to preserve their superior and deserving position, there is little likelihood that intimate and respectful relationships with partners can be developed.

Replacement of abusive beliefs with respectful beliefs is a prerequisite to respectful intimate relationships. This requires a model of *respectful relationship beliefs*. One such model is presented in Chapter 5.

5

Respectful Relationship Beliefs

To contrast with the belief systems of abusive men and to provide a direction for change, a model of respectful beliefs is required. This model needs to be one that supports and maintains respectful interactions between intimate partners, and one that promotes the equal individual development of each partner as well as the relationship itself.

The Stone Center at Wellesley College has pursued intensive investigations into the nature of relationships (Jordan et al., 1991). Initially, their work focused on understanding women's relationships, but there have been inevitable comparisons with relationships between men and consideration of women's relationships with men. Because there has been no investigation of relationship beliefs of nonabusive men, the present respectful relationship model is therefore derived largely from the study of relationships from women's perspectives. Because these perspectives are largely nonabusive and because women's investment in relationships is known to be greater than men's, this focus is not inappropriate.

Women have been denoted as "relationship experts," and studies confirm that women give greater importance to, invest more in, and are more skilled in sustaining relationships (Thompson & Walker, 1989; Williams, 1988). Contrary statements to the effect that men's relationship beliefs may be different but should be accorded equal value (Wood, 1993) cannot be supported, given the proclivity for such beliefs to support abusive and violent behavior.

Respectful relationship beliefs, then, are the converse of the relationship beliefs that support abuse. These beliefs include valuing *connection* as opposed to centrality and separation, valuing *equality* as opposed to superiority and dominance, and valuing *mutuality* rather than deservedness.

To foster respectful relationship beliefs in a therapeutic context and to encourage the replacement of abusive beliefs with respectful relationship beliefs, it is necessary to understand the origin of both sets of beliefs, the social contexts in which they have been developed, and the direction of therapy that such beliefs suggest.

❏ The Gendered Nature of Relationship Beliefs

Men and women are socialized from infancy to regard relationships differently and to adjust their behavior accordingly. Jean Baker Miller (1991) describes the process of male early development as stressing separation and individuation. Chodorow (1978) describes the male developmental process as "differentiating *from* relationship." Studies have indicated that compared to women, men are less empathic (Hoffman, 1977) and invest less and care less about close relationships (Thompson & Walker, 1989; Williams, 1988). Sadly, this emphasis on separation and the corresponding belief in the separate self can be overdeveloped as it is with abusive men, so that the other is totally disregarded.

Female socialization, in contrast, stresses connection and relatedness. Women's development, it has been suggested, is best explained by self-in-relation theory, which holds that the basic goal of development is a deepening capacity for relationship and relational competence (Surrey, 1991). Research data and clinical observation have provided evidence of women's greater ability for relatedness, emotional closeness, and emotional flexibility. This kind of connection in relationships, including the development of a highly complex ability to empathize with others, discourages abuse of the other or causing others pain.

Male socialization further stresses competition and dominance (Doyle, 1983; Pasick, 1990). Jordan (1991) describes how male stereotyped expectations regarding dominance and submission infuse all their relationships, including those with their female partners. These expectations tend to preclude the attainment of intimacy and promote abusiveness when such expectations are not met.

Equal male-female relationships are less prone to violence and abuse.

Female socialization, in contrast, stresses cooperation and equality (Gilligan, 1982; Miller, 1986). Surrey (1991) suggests that women's development moves from a relationship of caretaking (as in care of children) to one of consideration, caring, and empowering (as children mature). Relationships of inequality, therefore, are perceived as temporary with the potential of movement toward the desired goal of equal, more mature relationships. Equal male-female relationships are less prone to violence and abuse than are those based on inequality (Yllö, 1984).

Men are socialized in adulthood to expect their female partners to take care of their emotional needs (Pasick, Gordon, & Meth, 1990). Weiss (1990) describes marriage as the relationship to which men look for emotional and logistic support. Pleck (1983) notes that men perceive their heterosexual relationships as the only legitimate source of emotional support. Women are expected to soothe men's wounds and replenish their emotional resources. Adrienne Rich (1979) describes this expectation of emotional and sexual services from women and the expectation of women's undivided attention in any and all situations as "husband-right." This expectation of unidirectional care, nurturance, and support can become justification for abuse when expectations are not met (Ptacek, 1988).

Women's socialization, in contrast, stresses a belief in mutuality in relationships, where one affects and is affected by the other, where one extends oneself out to the other and is receptive to the effect of the other, and where there is emotional availability and constantly changing patterns of receptivity and active initiative toward the other (Jordan, 1991). Both the individual and her relationships are considered to be continually changing as the mutual interchange and accommodation results in growth and development. With this belief in mutuality, both participants in the relationship take responsibility for the relationship and for the avoidance of abusiveness within it.

In summary, male socialization leads to relationship beliefs that can promote abusive behaviors. Women's socialization experiences, in contrast, develop beliefs in connection, equality, and mutuality that tend to preclude abusiveness in relationships. A model of respectful relationships, therefore, requires the incorporation of the latter set of beliefs.

❏ Respectful Beliefs and Behaviors

In the present context, of beliefs regarding men's relationships with their intimate partners, a respectful belief system can be said to include the following tenets:

- A belief in one's connectedness and interrelatedness with one's partner
- A belief that the partner is a unique and equal person, whose differences are perceived to be an asset in the relationship
- A belief in the necessity for mutual exchange in and responsibility for relationships

Respectful relationship behaviors that result from such beliefs can be described as follows:

Respectful relationship behaviors are behaviors that convey consideration for the partner as an equal and connect with her in a mutual fashion.

Respectful relationship beliefs and their consequences are presented in Table 5.1.

Table 5.1 Respectful Beliefs and Their Consequences

Respectful Belief	Consequence
Connectedness	Consideration of partner
	Sensitivity to effects of own behavior on others
Equality	Partner regarded as equal
	Valuing differences
	Respectful interaction
Mutual engagement	Giving as well as taking
	Being affected by others
	Changing through interaction with others

❑ **Summary**

Men and women are exposed to different socializing experiences regarding the value accorded and attention given to relationships. Respectful relationship beliefs have received greater emphasis in female than in male socialization. Female socialization develops beliefs in relationship connectedness, equality, and mutual engagement. These beliefs inhibit abusive behaviors.

Respectful beliefs promote the equal growth and development of each partner.

Respectful relationship beliefs promote the equal growth and development of each partner in a relationship. Change is perceived as an integral part of relationships with the aim of such change being increasing respect and intimacy.

Because abusive men's social contexts typically have fostered abusive beliefs, changing such beliefs requires an alternate type of context. The therapeutic context provides an alternate milieu that promotes the exploration and confrontation of socially pervasive beliefs. Reinforcement for newly developing beliefs as well as confrontation of existing beliefs is best provided when the therapeutic context provides multiple supports and reinforcements. Therapeutic groups, rather than individual therapy, therefore, are considered the preferable medium of intervention.

PART III

Theory and Practice of Group Treatment

6

The Group as
the Medium of Change

Therapeutic groups provide a milieu in which men can examine their abusive beliefs and explore alternate beliefs that are denounced in their prevailing social contexts. The benefits of groups over individual therapy have been repeatedly observed when change in behaviors and expectations arising from abusive beliefs is sought.

A therapeutic group for abusive men that aims to alter beliefs provides a microcosm of an alternate social environment. This environment provides permission to challenge prevalent male beliefs, permission to engage in alternate ways of relating between men, and models of and opportunity for alternate ways of relating with women.

A uniquely different experience is provided in therapeutic groups for men who have generally not had opportunities to openly and honestly explore their beliefs about intimate relationships. This kind of self-exploration and self-confrontation is typically not fostered and therefore rare in male culture. Follow-up interviews with abusive men who have had the benefit of such an experience have revealed that group process and group support were consistently identified as the most important element in their change process (Gondolf, 1985; Tolman, 1990).

Prior to beginning a therapeutic group for abusive men, it is useful to have an understanding of the benefits and limitations of the group process. The benefits and challenges of a male therapist and a female therapist sharing group leadership need to be considered. In addition, the phases of the group process require some consideration.

❏ Benefits and Limitations of Abusive Men's Groups

Groups for abusive men provide opportunities for men that they are unlikely to have previously experienced. On entering the group, they are presented with the expectation of honest and open presentation of their behaviors, thoughts, and feelings to a group of their peers. The reinforcement of honesty and challenge to dissimulation provided by group members and leaders is likely to result in levels of self-disclosure, self-examination, and self-confrontation not previously experienced. Furthermore, the commonality of abuse and the common desire to eliminate it and establish respectful relations reduces individual isolation.

Groups, as opposed to individual therapy, provide numerous sources of input and feedback (Rose, 1989). Men in groups frequently can identify with the experiences of other group members, learning from the examples provided by others, talking and giving advice to others. Edleson and Tolman (1992) state that men derive particular benefits from their efforts in helping other group members. Not only does giving such help reinforce the man's own sense of competence, but it reinforces his own change process as he verbalizes his new awareness.

The emotional support that group members provide each other is particularly important as men begin to disclose thoughts, feelings, and behaviors that were previously kept hidden, especially from other men. These supportive interactions among group members can serve to decrease each man's dependence on his partner for emotional nurturance and support.

Support, encouragement, and reinforcement by other group members are beneficial when they are aimed at nonabusive beliefs and behaviors. As Hart (1988) has noted, however, such encouragement is also often provided for abusiveness, particularly in early group sessions. Frequently, men join with other group members in condemning partners and justifying abusiveness on the basis of the partner's "reprehensible" behaviors. Challenging the appropriateness of such encouragement or questioning how

> *It is acceptable to break taboos and challenge beliefs associated with masculinity.*

such beliefs will assist men in stopping their abuse is then required. The need for group leaders who are active and vigilant in this regard is paramount.

❑ Groups and the Belief Change Process

Therapeutic groups have been considered particularly powerful mechanisms for belief change (Nicholas, 1984). In the present context, the group environment provides men with an alternate social environment that supports and sustains belief change. With an aim of changing abusive beliefs, the group environment makes it acceptable to break taboos and challenge beliefs associated with masculinity. It is acceptable, in such groups, to admit that men's abusive beliefs lead to actions resulting in guilt, shame, and regret. It is acceptable for men to admit that their abusive beliefs fail to bring about the relationship outcomes they desire. Furthermore, it is acceptable and even desirable for men to voice beliefs and evidence behaviors that are contrary to prevailing notions of masculinity. The alternate environment of these groups is designed to nurture the belief modification process.

Group interactions tend to foster honest expressions of beliefs because the rate of interaction between members tends to be rapid, thereby limiting individual tendencies for self-censorship. Particularly when the discussion is heated and individual motivation to participate is high, spontaneous expressions of beliefs are frequent. These spontaneous expressions in turn lead to increased likelihood of confrontation of beliefs by self or others.

Confrontations of a stated or implied belief may come from multiple directions in a group. As group cohesion increases, the number of such confrontations is also likely to increase. Yalom (1975) describes such challenges as indispensable in producing change and notes the necessity of developing group cohesion so challenges can readily occur.

> *A female and male co-leading team is essential.*

In summary, therapeutic group experiences have been found to be particularly effective with abusive men. Change in men's beliefs about themselves and their place in relationships is particularly fostered in the group context. This change process is further facilitated by the presence of a female and male co-leading team.

❏ The Female Leader

A female and male co-leading team is essential for this program, given abusive men's belief in the central self and tendency to disregard the effects of their actions on others. The participation of a female leader inhibits the tendency for a uniform masculine perspective to develop in an all-male group. The female leader, in a sense, embodies female victims and serves as a constant reminder that male actions affect women. Role-playing of abusive interactions and modeling and rehearsal of respectful interactions all become possible with the presence of a female co-leader.

DISRUPTING THE MALE CULTURE

Given male socialization, which neglects the development of connection, equality, and mutual engagement, an all-male group can be deficient in its consideration of effects of men's behavior on women. The dominance of a male perspective may simply be unquestioned without a female presence. Lack of consideration of women's perspectives and tendencies to ignore or dismiss women can simply go unnoted. In contrast, a female leader can voice her perspective when it differs from the men's; she can express her feelings when she is ignored or her opinions are dismissed; she can note the behavior of group members who direct their comments exclusively to the male leader or ignore her questions.

The importance of a woman's presence in the group was remarked on by a group member:

> There is something about a male culture that gets broken down when you have a female intruder, you know, a certain aspect of keeping it between us guys.

EMBODYING THE ABUSED PARTNER

A female leader can function instrumentally to provide a constant reminder of the effects of abuse. In role plays, the female leader clearly enacts the effects of being abused. In addition, during group interactions, reflections by the female leader about how described abusive behaviors would affect her serve to remind group participants of the consequences of their actions. Coming from a woman, these reflections have more credibility than they would have from a male leader. Observations from a group member indicate the importance of these reminders:

> The female leader embodied for us a female presence that represented our partner. She was more credibly able to raise questions about how our behavior affected our partners.

MODELING AND PRACTICING
RESPECTFUL FEMALE-MALE RELATIONS

Considerable planning by group leaders is required to ensure that they consistently model equal and respectful behaviors. Constant vigilance is required by the leaders so that they avoid perpetuating their sex roles stereotypes. Planning for each session can ensure that tasks and responsibilities are shared equally. For example, in the early, more structured sessions, leaders can alternate introducing each new topic or activity. Monitoring levels of activity may be necessary to ensure that equality is retained over the course of the program. A basic commitment to equality by both the female leader and the male leader is essential.

A female leader can also encourage individual group members to practice respectful behaviors. For example, she can role-play a man's partner in a scenario in which he replaces his previous abusive behavior with a new behavior that conveys consideration and respect toward the partner.

CHALLENGES RELATED TO FEMALE CO-LEADING

Abusive men with limited experience in respectful relations with women may replicate their abusive behaviors in their interactions with the female leader. Overt hostility, sexual overtures, and dismissive actions are all likely to be displayed toward the female leader. Articulation of group norms that such behavior is unacceptable by both leaders generally serves to bring such behaviors to a halt.

Women's participation in a group for men that aims to increase men's responsibility for their own behavior can be viewed as a paradox. Men, it has been argued, should be solving their own problems without women's intervention. Although this argument has some merit, it is also clear that an abusive man's beliefs in his central, superior, and deserving self can be maintained quite comfortably until the female perspective intrudes. Given the pervasiveness and dominance of male belief systems, it is unlikely that much change can be engendered without a female protest, either on an individual basis as abusive men's partners protest their abusiveness or in a therapeutic context in which abusive beliefs and actions are challenged. Women's participation, therefore, is likely to be a necessary catalyst for some time to come.

❏ The Male Leader

Male leaders have an important function in developing a group milieu in which the exploration of beliefs in connectedness, equality, and mutual engagement is promoted. It is essential that the male leader is himself committed to such beliefs and is open to confrontation when his behavior is not consistent with such beliefs. The male leader can demonstrate the continuous nature of belief confrontation by describing his own change process. He can describe the social forces that act as barriers to the process of belief change and his own struggles with overcoming beliefs in his centrality, superiority, and deservedness. The male leader can engage in a dialogue with the female leader regarding the importance of equality and mutual responsibility for their interactions and group functioning. At all times, the male leader needs to remember to reinforce connectedness, equality, and mutual engagement.

Connectedness can be demonstrated by the male leader through his interest in and concern for the experiences of the female co-leader in the group. Following role plays, for example, the male leader can encourage discussion about the female leader's experience of being abused. Through demonstrating his own interest in her experiences, he can encourage group members to be aware of and develop empathy with the female leader, and by association, their own partners' experiences in being abused.

The male leader also demonstrates connectedness through taking an active stance against disregard for or disrespect shown to the female leader. The male leader's role, in this respect, is not to be a protector of the female leader, but her ally in clarifying group norms regarding behavior toward women.

Demonstrating his commitment to equality in the group is essential. This involves an equal sharing of all aspects of group leadership as well as being sensitive to male interactions that exclude the female. Vigilance is required by the male leader to restrain tendencies, developed through male socialization, to dominate the group. In addition, he should be prepared to have such behavior confronted by the female leader or other group members.

Mutual engagement with the female leader requires that the male leader acknowledge that her insights have provided a perspective from which he can benefit personally and professionally. Demonstration by the male leader that he benefits from his increased understanding of the female perspective is essential if this kind of receptivity is to be fostered in group members.

In summary, the male and female leaders, through their own commitment to connection, equality, and mutuality, provide an environment in which these beliefs are fostered. The group process that evolves, therefore, is infused with these beliefs, and group members are clearly expected to act in accordance with them. The respectful nature of the group process that ensues can serve as a model for interactions in other relationships.

❑ The Group Process

Abusive men's progression through the group program can be conceptualized as consisting of four stages: *setting the stage, confronting abusive beliefs, developing respectful beliefs,* and *consolidating changed beliefs.* Although the program is structured to promote change in this sequence, individual men vary considerably in the rate that they become aware of their abusive beliefs and the extent to which they confront and alter such beliefs.

The entire group process, furthermore, tends to be reiterative rather than linear. There tends to be a regular and continuous return to prior issues, usually with more understanding of the complexities of these issues. Repetition of this kind is generally constructive in both reinforcing previous learning and in aiding the integrating new beliefs.

Setting the stage, or explaining parameters and clarifying expectations of the group process, is a vital component of group process. Stockton and Moran (1982) review evidence of numerous studies of group outcome that indicates that structuring of early group sessions to provide information and a sense of safety for group members promotes the development of group cohesion and productive subsequent functioning. Active participation by group leaders in this initial stage permits group members to observe group process and become acclimatized to group norms without taking excessive risks. Initial self-disclosures by group members can be structured to be factual and brief so that while reinforcing the expectation of disclosures, the depth of disclosure is left as the group member's choice. In short, considerable structuring and active leader participation in the first phase of the group process provides the conditions that are conducive to exploration and confrontation of beliefs in subsequent phases.

Confronting abusive beliefs, the second group phase, requires a balance of support and challenge. Early termination or dropout is a significant problem in abusive men's groups (Grusznski & Carrillo, 1988; Saunders, 1992). Discomfort at confrontations presented too early may be partially implicated in some of these terminations. Conversely, however, abusive men are likely to have partners whose safety may be at risk. Statements of abusive beliefs or other statements that indicate that a partner's safety is in peril cannot go unchallenged.

A useful method for confronting abusive beliefs at this stage of the group process is the enactment of role plays by the group leaders. These role plays serve to demonstrate and externalize abusive beliefs and their outcomes, without directly challenging individual group participants. Group members typically can identify with the abusive actions and be more sensitive to effects of abuse on the female when they are in the role of observer.

Directing questions to group participants that encourage self-exploration, or presenting them with challenging questions, is another useful and relatively unthreatening method for belief confrontation at this stage of the process. These questions can be directed either at individuals or the group as a whole. An immediate answer to the questions is not necessary; some questions are better simply aired with the expectation that group members will consider these questions between group sessions. Indicating that the beliefs challenged are socially prevalent and that individual adherence to such beliefs is understandable given their social milieu allows individuals to take a more detached perspective on their beliefs. Identifying that socially prevalent beliefs may be inimical to development of respectful relationships allows individuals to reevaluate these beliefs without feeling personally attacked.

Self-exploration and reevaluation of beliefs during this phase is likely to create anxiety and discomfort in group participants. In reconsidering entrenched beliefs, group members may indicate that they feel adrift, having lost their customary, traditional benchmarks about their place in relationships. Group leaders can assist in reframing this confusion as a positive indication of change, a necessary but uncomfortable accompaniment to personal growth, and provide reassurance that this degree of discomfort is temporary. The discomfort of this phase is alleviated by the replacement of abusive beliefs with more respectful beliefs in the next phase.

Development of respectful beliefs begins during the third phase of the process in which reevaluation of previously discredited beliefs and new learning takes place. Abusive men may have rejected respectful relationship beliefs because these have been viewed as unmasculine. A reformulation of a positive image of masculinity that incorporates respectful beliefs, therefore, may be necessary. For example, group attendance and disclosure of abuse can be redefined as acts of courage. Coping with negative emotions oneself, rather than projecting blame and anger on one's partner, can be redefined as an act of strength. Listening to one's partner and acknowledging the validity of her perspective can be defined as mature and respectful behavior. Caring for others can be reformulated as evidence of strength, maturity, and courage.

The group process is invaluable in developing and supporting new respectful beliefs. Examples provided by group leaders and group members provide models and reinforcement for the development of such beliefs. Group support is particularly critical when group members lack other sources of support for respectful beliefs in their social contexts.

Consolidation of respectful beliefs represents the terminal or ending phase of the group process. This phase involves a review of progress to date as well as making concrete plans for the future. Termination also includes acknowledgment that the group environment supported belief change and that alternate supportive resources are now required. Finding support among other like-minded men is frequently one of the important outcomes of this phase of group process.

❑ Summary

Therapeutic groups provide a powerful medium for the process of belief confrontation and alteration. Men's abusive beliefs are subject to confrontation and challenge in an environment that encourages the expression and enactment of alternate respectful belief systems. Men's beliefs about women and their relationship with women become apparent and subject to confrontation through a process that involves a female as well as a male leader. Recognition that belief change is fostered through a process that consolidates support and challenge, self-examination and new learning, leads to consideration of structure and format of the group process.

7

Group Formation and Structure

Producing change in abusive men's belief systems through a therapeutic group program requires consideration of group formation and structure. Selection criteria for a program that aims at belief change need to ensure that a possibility of such change exists. Multipurpose assessment procedures have been developed that not only aim to screen applicants but also engage them in a dialogue that initiates the belief change process.

Program structure has been designed to further such belief change through activities that promote awareness and encourage examination of belief systems.

Guidelines and structures are suggested with the recognition of the overriding concern for the safety of abusive men's partners. This concern is foremost during assessment as well as throughout the group program.

❏ Assessment Criteria

This program was designed for men who limit their abusiveness largely to their female partners and are not generally violent. Because the program aims to confront individual belief systems that pertain to intimate relationships, it may have less applicability for men whose violence is more generalized. When more generally violent men have participated in this program, it has usually been found necessary to emphasize behavioral components of the program.

A capacity for self-examination and a preparedness to evaluate one's belief system are requisites for the program. This in turn requires at least the capability to conceive of the possibility of changing beliefs. Men whose belief systems are highly entrenched, who are resistant to self-examination or change, or who have little support for or motivation to change are at high risk of early termination in this program. Although such men should not necessarily be excluded, an assessment procedure that makes the program requirements explicit allows the men to make an informed choice about participation. Men who suffer from mental or substance abuse disorders have been found to be limited in their capacity to fully participate in the program.

In short, the selection criteria for this program are the following:

- Abusive behavior limited to female partner(s)
- Willingness to disclose abuse and examine beliefs
- Lack of serious disorders (e.g., mental, substance abuse)

❏ Assessment Procedure

Separate interviews with the abusive man and his partner are conducted to elicit information about the abuse and to provide information about group programs. For abusive men, the interview presents the opportunity to become engaged in a dialogue regarding the appropriateness of the program for him at this time. For the partner who has been abused, the interview provides the opportunity to focus on her needs for safety, for action to remedy the damaging effects of the abuse, and to confront any expressed beliefs that she might be responsible for the abuse that she suffered.

MEN'S ASSESSMENT

There are two primary objectives in the men's assessments. The first is to obtain information about his perception of the nature and extent of his abuse and about his receptivity to viewing abusiveness in a different fashion. Information about the presence of other disorders is also obtained. The second purpose is to prepare the man for group participation by informing him about the nature of the group program. In this way, the man and the interviewer engage in a dialogue that permits an informed decision regarding his participation in the program to be made.

Statements made by the man regarding the severity of the abuse and the effects of the abuse on his partner provide an indication of the degree to which he subscribes to abusive relationship beliefs. A total inability or unwillingness to take responsibility for his actions or to consider consequences can indicate a lack of readiness for the group program.

Abusive men are known to minimize or trivialize their abusiveness and to shift the blame for the abuse onto their partners, particularly in initial discussions. This is to be expected in an assessment interview. Determination of suitability for group treatment, therefore, depends less on the initial descriptions of abuse and more on the willingness to or interest expressed in considering alternate conceptualizations and consequences of abuse. For example, when a man's belief that his partner "caused" him to be abusive is challenged by suggesting that his behavior is always a choice, his response provides an indication to his openness to change.

Persistence in blaming and total unwillingness to consider his responsibility for abusiveness can be taken as indicators of lack of suitability, and the man is informed of this. For example, the interviewer can state:

> This group is about men examining and changing their own behaviors and beliefs. I wonder, given what you have just said, if you are prepared to do that.

Men who are interested in personal change will generally respond in the affirmative, whereas those not interested in personal change will continue to blame and challenge.

Likewise, men who are unwilling to consider the effects of their actions on their partners may not be suitable group participants. Interviewers can gauge this level of willingness by making observations such as the following:

> I wonder what it is like for your partner, sleeping in the same bed with a man who has caused her so much pain.

> It must be difficult for your partner to trust you since you broke your promise to love and cherish her.

Responses that continue blaming the partner, or indicate a lack of willingness by the man to consider his partner's fear or mistrust, can be taken as negative indicators for successful group participation. Interviewers can indicate that the group program is based on the premise that men are 100% responsible for their actions and the

The group program is based on the premise that men are 100% responsible for their actions.

consequences thereof. If they are unwilling to examine consequences, the program may not be suitable for them.

Willingness to assume responsibility, and openness to considering alternate explanations for abuse, in contrast, are to be reinforced during the assessment interview. Men who acknowledge their need to change are to be commended for their courage in acknowledging the consequences of their actions and taking responsibility for these. For example, the interviewer may state:

> It takes courage for a man to admit that he has caused his partner pain, and it is evidence of strength when he acknowledges that he needs to change. Such courage and strength are needed to successfully complete this program.

Information about the definitions of abuse, responsibility for abuse, and focus on examining men's beliefs and actions is provided as part of the assessment process. The definition of abuse used in the program includes psychological, economic, and sexual abuse in addition to physical abuse, and it is important to convey that this range of behaviors will be considered. Men frequently expect only to discuss incidents of serious physical violence, and the assessment, therefore, provides the opportunity to engage them in considering a wider range of their behaviors and the implications of those behaviors.

Consideration of effects of abuse on partners is described as an essential program component and a necessary prerequisite to producing comprehensive and sustained behavior change. Involving the man in a dialogue regarding his perception of such consequences is useful in initiating this process and providing a preview of group process.

Reinforcement of the notion of consequences can also be provided by asking the man to describe what actions he can take immediately to ensure his partner's safety. Information about "time out," described in Session 1, can be provided at this time as one method of demonstrating concern for his partner's safety.

PARTNERS' ASSESSMENT

Assessment interviews with the partners who have been abused are desirable, but dependent on the willingness of the partner to be involved. Many partners indicate that they have no desire for further communication or discussion regarding the abusive man, and these wishes must be respected. When a partner is willing to participate, interviewers must be cognizant of any threats to her safety and address any concerns of this nature during the interview.

The aim in interviewing the partner is to obtain and validate her perception of the abuse, to provide recognition of effects of abuse on her and any children involved, and to emphasize the necessity of continuing vigilance regarding her own safety. Recognition and validation of the seriousness and effect of abuse on the partner and the children is essential because these consequences have frequently been dismissed or trivialized by others. It may be difficult for the partner to acknowledge or articulate effects of repeated abusive devaluation of her competencies and abilities. Her social context may regard abusive men's actions as normal, resulting in confusion about the validity of her own experiences and perceptions. Furthermore, in aiming to gain some sense of control over her own life, she may accept responsibility for abuse. By perceiving herself responsible, she gains hope that she can eliminate the abuse through her own actions.

Information that places the responsibility for the abuse with the abuser is conveyed during the interview with the partner. Beliefs in shared blame or responsibility for abuse are countered by emphasizing individual choice in behavior. In addition, expected consequences of receiving abuse, such as a diminished sense of self and personal identity, are explained. Information about resources for women who have been abused is provided.

Continued vigilance regarding her own safety is described as necessary because men's group participation, although generally reducing rates of violence and abuse, provides no guarantee that such reduction will occur for any given man. Partners who are in the process of separating or have recently separated from the abusive man are informed of the elevated risk of abuse during this period.

Participation in a support group for women is encouraged for partners who indicate difficulty in dealing with the effects of abuse. The benefits of being part of a supportive environment with women who have had similar experiences is described.

In conclusion, assessment is regarded as the beginning of a dialogue that raises awareness of beliefs and suggests the direction of change. Although the primary focus is on the men as potential group participants, the process also aims to involve partners and to encourage them to care for themselves. For the men, the process begun during assessment is structured to continue throughout the group program.

❏ Group Composition

An ideal group size is one that allows for maximum group interaction and cohesion but takes into account the likelihood of attrition. Groups that initially are composed of 12 to 14 men will generally evolve into a cohesive and enduring group of 7 to 10 men. The more rigorous the initial screening and assessment, the less likelihood of early termination.

❏ Program Structure

NUMBER OF SESSIONS

The suggested format of 12 weekly group sessions allows for presentation and group interaction in relation to each program topic. Given diverse rates of progress through the group by group members, a follow-up group for those wishing to continue has proven to be the preferable option as compared to extending groups beyond 12 sessions.

Each session is of 2½ hours' duration, including one 15-minute midpoint break. Monitoring the length of activities, such as the check-in, and curtailing those of undue length is frequently necessary. Although this may limit participation by particular group members, the group derives the benefit of moving forward.

STRUCTURE OF SESSIONS

All sessions, excluding the first and last, have a similar structure. The aim of this structure is to provide a balance between individual self-disclosures, group interactions, and presentation of new material by group leaders. The format for each of these sessions includes the following:

- Check-in by each group member in turn
- Topic presentation, which includes
    handouts
    challenging questions
  and may involve
    didactic presentations
    role plays
    brainstorming exercises
- Check-out by each member in turn
- Distribution of reflections logs

Check-In

During the check-in, each group member in turn describes an event during the past week in which he was abusive or avoided becoming abusive. During the check-in, each man is asked to describe his actions, thoughts, and feelings during the event as well as the effects of his actions on others. The aim in disclosing such events is for each man to be more aware and take more responsibility for abuse. In addition, reinforcement for avoiding abuse is provided by group leaders and group members.

The importance of honesty and openness in the check-in is stressed. The discomfort that men experience in disclosing abusiveness is acknowledged. This discomfort is redefined as a positive indicator, a necessary accompaniment to individual growth and change.

Group members are instructed to listen carefully and ask questions for clarification only as other members are checking in. Questioning and dialogue frequently must be curtailed so that each group member receives adequate time for his check-in. Listening is described as a respectful behavior, and respectful questioning, likewise, is promoted. The format for the check-in is outlined in Handout 6.

Leader Functions During Check-In

Leaders begin the check-in by inviting members to begin and reminding them of the procedure. Leaders then monitor the time, focus, topics, and stated or implied beliefs of each disclosure.

Monitoring time and focus is particularly important in the early group sessions. A rule of thumb in early sessions is to limit each person to 5 minutes. Respecting the rights of other group members requires that each man take responsibility for making a succinct presentation. Likewise, showing respect for the agreed-on purpose of the group requires that each man focus on his own thoughts, feelings, and actions and not those of his partner. Leader intervention is required when men begin to describe or complain about partner's actions.

Monitoring topics raised and beliefs implicit in men's statements during check-in provides leaders with important links to program content. These links can be noted and integrated into the subsequent topic presentation. For example, the recurrent theme in the men's disclosures that they expect to dominate relationships can easily be integrated into topics such as self-monitoring, consequences of abuse, or others. Some topics or implied beliefs, however, may require more immediate response. For example, a man who states that he became abusive because his partner pushed his buttons requires a response that questions his belief that his partner controls and is therefore responsible for his actions.

Similarly, responses or questions from group members that deflect the focus to the partner, blame the partner, or indicate a belief that the partner was responsible for the abuse requires an immediate response. Group leaders can respond by asking the individual or the group as a whole whether such responses are likely to be helpful to them in overcoming their abusiveness.

As group process develops and as men become more comfortable and practiced in disclosing and responding to disclosures, group leaders can become more active in making connections between disclosures and content of sessions. In later group sessions, the check-in may become more of a dialogue or group interaction that consumes increasingly greater portions of each session. Leaders, however, must ensure that all group members are provided with the opportunity to check in each week and to disclose any abuse that may have occurred during the week.

In summary, leader functions during check-in include the following:

- Encouraging open, honest, and detailed accounts of abusiveness.
- Monitoring focus to ensure it remains on the man's actions, thoughts, or feelings.
- Redirecting focus if it shifts to behavior of partners or others.
- Acknowledging men's courage in disclosing abusiveness.
- Praising actions taken to avoid abusiveness.
- Monitoring time limits for each presentation and noting when these have been exceeded.
- Noting common themes for integration into topic presentation.
- Noting responses by group members that minimize, dismiss, or trivialize abuse and pointing these out to the group.
- Thanking each man for his check-in.

Topic Presentation

Each session has at least one suggested topic. These topics have been ordered so that there is progressively more intense self-examination required. There is also a progressive emphasis from abusive to respectful beliefs. The initial topics are structured to examine beliefs related to the central self that allow men to define their actions as nonabusive and to ignore the consequences of their behavior. Subsequent topics focus on the belief in the superior self and deserving self, how these beliefs affect their expectations of and interactions with their partners, and how they are used to justify abusiveness. Initial emphasis on abusive beliefs becomes modified as the program advances to a greater emphasis on development, implementation, and reinforcement of respectful beliefs.

Because group members progress at different rates and present their own concerns at different points, flexibility in sequencing of presentations is recommended. Leaders need to be familiar with all topics so that each can be introduced as appropriate. In some sessions, it may be necessary to discuss several topics, making reference to those presented earlier as well as those yet to come. Each group is, furthermore, unique in terms of its requirements. Some groups will require several repetitions of a specific topic, whereas others may require only a cursory overview of a given topic. Leader judgment and sensitivity to group needs is essential.

Presentation of each topic is supplemented by prepared handouts and challenging questions.

Handouts. The purpose of handouts is to present the essence of the topic presentation in a form that promotes further self-exploration and examination of beliefs. Some handouts are designed as exercises that can be completed either during or between group sessions. Some men have used handouts effectively to initiate dialogue with their partners. However, men should be cautioned about inviting such discussion because partners may not feel sufficiently safe to voice their opinions or thoughts. A partner's wishes regarding such discussions need to be respected.

Challenging Questions. The purpose of challenging questions is to elicit underlying beliefs, bring beliefs to awareness, and confront men with consequences of their beliefs. In particular, such questions aim to emphasize the consequences of abusive relationship beliefs or contrasting respectful beliefs on partners.

Questioning, as suggested by Jenkins (1990), is likely to avoid defensive reactions when presented as an invitation to participate in self-exploration and discovery. Abusive men can be invited to explore their belief systems and to make discoveries about the partner, including the effects of abusive actions on her. Promoting and reinforcing a curiosity about the self and the partner can be an effective way of increasing awareness and confronting beliefs.

Challenging questions can be directed to the group as a whole to promote group interaction and development of cohesion. Encouraging group members to reflect on or agree or disagree with each other's responses can provide useful feedback to individual group members. For example, the group as a whole can be asked for responses to questions such as the following:

> When Joe insists that his partner caused him to be abusive, what does that suggest to you about his willingness to change?
>
> Several of you have mentioned that you believe your partner is inept in managing household finances, and arguments about finances often become abusive. Since this is a common problem, I wonder what lies behind it?

Examples of challenging questions are provided for each session in subsequent chapters.

Didactic Presentations. The purpose of didactic presentations is to introduce new information, new concepts, or new definitions to the group. Didactic presentations are most appropriate in early, more structured sessions where they provide group members with clear rules and expectations. In later sessions, didactic presentations can be more flexibly integrated with group process. For example, a brief didactic presentation about the benefits of equal relationships can be incorporated at the point when a man discovers that he has gained some insight by respectfully listening to her remarks.

Role Plays. A number of role plays have been developed for purposes of demonstrating abusiveness and portraying the effects on the partner. As the male leader enacts the abusive incident, group members are encouraged to note similarities with their own situation. As the female leader is subject to the abuse, group members are encouraged to note the effects of abusiveness on her and consider the parallels with their own partners.

Role plays that have been repeatedly proven useful are presented. However, role plays that depict a particular issue presented or the particular situation of one group member can provide a powerful stimulus for group discussion and examination of beliefs.

Brainstorming. The purpose of brainstorming is to provide maximum group participation in the generation and discussion of new concepts or definitions. This is particularly important when the intent is to broaden or expand the definition of a concept, such as abusiveness, or to sensitize group members to their own reactions or beliefs, as in self-monitoring. Brainstorming, as a structured activity, is also more appropriate in early group sessions.

During brainstorming, identification of as many examples as possible of a given concept is encouraged. Each group member is encouraged to identify at least one example. All examples are recorded without comment or judgment by leaders on a flip chart or blackboard. Discussion of examples and consideration of their commonalities or differences proceeds only after all responses have been exhausted.

Check-Out

The purpose of the check-out is for each group member to briefly indicate what he found to be of import during a particular group session. In this way, a brief review and reinforcement of the material presented can be made. Unresolved or negative reactions can be noted by group leaders and dealt with either after the group, between sessions, or incorporated into the material for the next session.

Reflections Logs

The purpose of reflections logs is to provide a mechanism for group members to review each week's group experience and connect it with their own situations. The reflections logs constitute the homework for the group and promote self-exploration during the interval between group sessions. Another, more secondary, purpose is to provide feedback to group leaders regarding the effect of group sessions.

Reflections logs are handed out at the end of each session and the completed ones are collected at the beginning of the next session. Handout 5 provides a sample of a weekly reflections log.

❏ Summary

Weekly sessions provide a sense of security and regularity for group members. This is particularly important in early group sessions, when likelihood of early termination is highest. Structure provides a sense of safety as expectations and rules are being defined. Flexibility increases and structure decreases as group cohesion develops and group members become more engaged in the process. Structured activities, likewise, are more appropriate for early group sessions. Checking in and out, however, remain important components of group structure throughout.

PART IV

Group Session Protocols

8

Setting the Stage: Sessions 1, 2, and 3

The therapeutic task in this first phase of the program is to provide conditions that will make the subsequent belief system change possible. These conditions include decreased anxiety about group participation, increased trust in the group, development of a common frame of reference, and development of group cohesion. These conditions will facilitate the development of group members' identification with and participation in the group process.

Accomplishment of these tasks is facilitated by providing a structured agenda for the first three sessions that involves a high degree of leader activity. Norms for group participation are clearly laid out by the leaders to clarify the behavioral expectations of each group member. Expectations regarding self-disclosures are structured and directed to be relatively nonthreatening in this early phase.

During the first session, a proposed program is outlined and group members are invited to suggest changes or modifications. The aim is to engage group members in a dialogue in which they begin to accept some responsibility for a productive group process. Although not many suggestions are typically received, the message that group process depends on contributions of members is one that is introduced and is reiterated throughout the program.

The format of the first three sessions is provided in considerable detail, with explicit directions for leaders. Experience with the program has indicated that little variation is generally required in the format of these early sessions. The structure of these sessions has been found to meet group members' need for information and reassurance about the group process.

Each session will be described in terms of goals, outlines, and detailed agenda.

Session 1: Introduction to the Group

❑ **Goals**

- Welcome group members and acknowledge courage demonstrated through attendance.
- Provide information about group format and process.
- Begin developing group cohesion through inviting suggestions regarding program content and requesting initial structured disclosures.

❑ **Outline**

Introductory remarks
Introduction of group leaders and members
Purpose of group: Handout 1
Group format
Participant agreement: Handout 2
Initial self-disclosure: Handout 3
Time out: Handout 4

Distribute reflections logs: Handout 5
Check-out

❏ Detailed Agenda for Session 1

INTRODUCTORY REMARKS

Welcoming remarks by both group leaders aim to make group members feel comfortable. Leaders acknowledge the courage required to admit abusive behavior and to take steps to change such behaviors. It is noted that attending the present program signifies a willingness to change and to take personal risks. It can be noted that men generally find it difficult to acknowledge and take responsibility for relationship problems.

The unique nature of the present program in providing an opportunity for men to connect and interact in ways that are generally not available can be described. It can be noted that an opportunity for group members to describe their experiences and express emotions in ways that they might be reluctant to do in other settings will be provided. The benefit that men in previous groups have derived from such an experience can be described.

An overview of observed program outcomes can be presented. Noting that group participants commonly report significantly decreased levels of violence and abuse during group participation generally serves to instill hope in new members. Furthermore, noting that group completers generally report improved ways of thinking about and relating to female partners provides an indication of the expected direction of change. A forewarning can be given that group participation may result in feelings of confusion and increased distress. However, group members can be reassured that these are generally temporary and are, in fact, indications of personal growth and change. Leaders can further acknowledge that individuals are likely to feel awkward and embarrassed during the first few sessions. It can be noted that by program completion most members are sad to disperse, indicating that the process has been a positive experience.

INTRODUCTION OF GROUP
LEADERS AND MEMBERS

Leader Introductions

Group leaders begin by providing brief introductions of themselves, their backgrounds, and their experience. Group leaders may wish to speak of their own experiences with violence and abuse to provide some personal context to their remarks.

Reference by both leaders to their commitment to an egalitarian working relationship is useful. Leaders may note that sometimes this is a struggle, given their own sex role socialization. This message conveys to group members the expectation of gender equality within the group, as well as noting that efforts toward equality are an ongoing process.

The female and male leaders also describe their different functions in the group. The female leader may note that some men initially experience discomfort at a woman's presence in the group. She can explain that this is a normal reaction given that she, in some ways, embodies the presence of their partners. The importance of a female who reminds group members that their relationship behaviors have consequences is emphasized. The female leader can reiterate that program completers have uniformly indicated that a female presence is beneficial.

The male leader can speak of his own experiences that are similar to those of group members as being part of a culture that values male dominance and superiority. He can describe the extent to which he was inculcated into prevailing belief systems that shape men's behavior and indicate how this affected his relationships. He can also describe the benefits he personally has derived from reevaluation of beliefs and adoption of respectful beliefs.

Group Member Introductions

Each group member is asked to briefly introduce himself, giving his first name and some relatively impersonal information such as place of residence. This process may need to be repeated as late arrivals join the group.

PURPOSE OF THE GROUP

(Distribute Handout 1.) The purpose of the group and the pre-
sumed common goal of group members is to eliminate abusive
behavior. The way to reach this goal is through understanding what
constitutes abuse, what kinds of beliefs support abuse, and how
these beliefs can be replaced by ones that support respectful behaviors in relationships. These program components are listed in Handout 1 and can be addressed individually by group leaders as a way
of introduction to the group.

It is important for leaders to emphasize that the focus of the
program is on *men's* abusive actions and beliefs. Women's abusive
acts are not considered because such consideration does not help
men to deal with their own abusiveness. Frequently, men will persist
in diverting focus from themselves to their partners. Challenging
questions such as the following can be helpful in returning the focus
onto the men:

> How does discussing your partner's behavior help or hinder you in
> changing your thoughts or actions?

In contrast, it is important to note that the *effect* of men's abusiveness
on women does require attention. Without awareness of consequences of abuse, bringing about fundamental belief change may
prove difficult.

Group members are encouraged to respond to and engage in discussion regarding the extent to which the questions in Handout 1
address their concerns. Suggestions for additional topics can be solicited. Typically, responses include topics such as dealing with anger,
stress management, and jealousy. A useful response is that these
topics will be dealt with in the context of beliefs supporting
abuse. If topics are suggested that relate to women's behavior,
group leaders again need to emphasize the group focus on men's
abusiveness.

GROUP FORMAT

Having reached agreement regarding group purpose, leaders provide basic information about format such as beginning and ending

times, time allotted for a break, scheduling of sessions, and regula-
tions for use of facility (e.g., smoking, parking). Again, group members can be asked to give responses to those aspects of the format
that are negotiable.

PARTICIPANT AGREEMENT

(Distribute Handout 2.) The participant agreement is introduced
as a proposed contract between group members. It spells out the expectations and responsibilities of group members in terms of nature
of participation, confidentiality, and responsible attendance. It is
useful for group leaders to read out the agreement and spend some
time addressing each point as members are likely to find several
discomforting.

Confidentiality is a principle that may require more extensive
discussion. In most jurisdictions, there are legal requirements regarding safety of others that override professional considerations of client-
therapist confidentiality. These must be noted.

Confidentiality between group members also requires discussion.
Some members may consider their participation in the group to be
of a confidential nature. For example, some group members may not
wish to acknowledge other group members outside the confines of
the group. This issue may, therefore, require some discussion as
group members indicate their wishes in this regard and other group
members make a commitment to respect those wishes.

Suggestions for amendments or additions to the group agreement
can be solicited. When all parties are comfortable with the agreement,
each group member is asked to sign his copy and have his signature
witnessed by another group member. This process reinforces the
responsibility of each group member to the larger constituency of
the group.

INITIAL SELF-DISCLOSURE

(Distribute Handout 3.) Seven questions were prepared to structure the initial self-disclosure; this tends to be a particularly anxiety-
producing experience. Most of the questions can be answered in a
factual manner without a great degree of elaboration.

As group leaders introduce this activity, they can acknowledge the difficult nature of this task. Men are typically not expected or willing to disclose the nature and extent of their abuse. Describing effects of abuse, per Question 3, may be particularly difficult because it is the aspect of abuse that men would most like to forget. Probes that can be used if men are unable to address this topic include the following examples:

> Do you now see signs of fear in your partner's face whenever you raise your voice (or your hand)?
>
> Does your partner now seem afraid to contradict or question you in any way?

Full disclosure of abuse, including extent of injuries or other consequences, can be promoted by noting that maintaining secrecy about these events is an impediment to change. If the problems are not discussed and considered in full, it is unlikely that a complete resolution can be obtained.

Partners should be referred to by name.

Group members are instructed to listen carefully and respectfully to each other's disclosures. Questions are to be asked for clarification only. Instruction may be given that partners should be referred to by name because this is a way of demonstrating respect.

Disrespectful references to partners require immediate intervention. Challenging questions such as the following can be posed in response:

> What does your referring to your partner in that way indicate about your level of respect for her?
>
> Does referring to your partner in that way make it easier or more difficult for you to be abusive toward her?

At the conclusion of each man's disclosure, both group leaders can thank him, as an important gesture of respect. Group leaders can note when the disclosure was particularly difficult for a group member and can reiterate that he has demonstrated courage and initiated the change process through his disclosures.

TIME OUT

(Distribute Handout 4.) As many group members are anxious to acquire some behavioral guidelines to avoid abuse, the time-out procedure that was introduced during the assessment is reviewed.

Men's responsibility for avoiding abusive action is emphasized. It can be noted that if men are serious about changing their abusive behaviors, then taking a time out is one way of beginning such change.

Reviewing the steps involved in the process, emphasizing men's responsibility to leave the situation can be useful. It can be noted that leaving, however, must be done in a specified manner that has been previously discussed with the partner. Time out is a tool to avoid abuse in a crisis situation. It is not to be used as a way of avoiding communication with the partner.

Use of a time out can be described as a display of strength. It takes considerably more strength to avoid abuse than to become abusive. Contrary to general notions that avoidance is equivalent to "wimping out," behaving respectfully is not only more courageous but also more beneficial in the long run.

DISTRIBUTE REFLECTIONS LOGS

(Distribute Handout 5.) Reflections logs are the required homework for each session. The purpose of the reflections logs is to promote review and consolidation of weekly topics. Each man is asked to reflect back on what he found particularly helpful in the group and how he can apply it to his own situation. A comment on what could have been more helpful is also requested. In this way, the logs provide information that can be used to modify content or process according to the needs of group members.

CHECK-OUT

As a closing exercise in each session, each group member in turn is asked to indicate what was particularly useful or relevant to him in the session. The purpose is to encourage reflection and integration, as well as to identify any areas that may require attention between sessions or in the next session.

Session 2: Definitions of Abuse and Respect

❑ **Goals**

- Develop a comprehensive definition of abuse.
- Label own abusive behaviors as such by each group member.

❑ **Outline**

Collect reflections logs
Check-in: Handout 6
Feedback about time out
Abusive behaviors: Handout 7
Definitions of abuse and respect: Handout 8
Distribute reflections logs: Handout 5
Check-out

❑ **Detailed Agenda for Session 2**

COLLECT REFLECTIONS LOGS

In this first collection of reflections logs, it is important to comment on the benefits of completing the logs on a regular basis as a review of progress. Thanking those group members who have completed the logs and asking them to describe how they have benefited can be used to encourage other group members who did not complete their logs.

CHECK-IN

(Distribute Handout 6.) As a follow-up to self-disclosures in the first session, the check-in as the regular weekly procedure is introduced. The purpose of this weekly check-in is described as providing each group member with an uninterrupted period of time to describe an event in his life during the past week that was relevant to his abuse. Group members are asked to describe an incident in which they *chose* to behave in an abusive fashion or *chose* to avoid becoming abusive. Their descriptions are expected to be specific and to detail their actions, thoughts, and the effects of their actions on others.

Other group members are instructed to listen carefully and to ask questions for clarification only.

Group leader functions regarding the check-in are as follows:

- Reviewing the process to ensure that all group members are clear about the format.
- Monitoring time limits, generally allowing no more than 5 minutes per person.
- Ensuring that the focus remains on the group member when abusive actions or thoughts are described. More detail in the description can be requested when a tendency to avoid or minimize is apparent.
- Ensuring that effects of the abuse are described. The female group leader can encourage increased consideration of effects by remarking how such behavior would have affected her.
- Ensuring that questions from group members are brief and limited to clarification.

Challenging Questions

During the check-in, it is likely that group members will demonstrate their belief that they are not totally responsible for their abusive acts. Challenging questions that can be posed to confront this belief include the following:

How does your justifying your abuse by saying she provoked you help or hinder you in making changes in yourself?

How does describing yourself as a victim affect your ability to make changes?

Also, group members may pose questions in a manner that indicate a similar belief on their part—for example, "Did she hit you first?" Questions such as the following can be posed to the group to challenge such expressions of belief:

How does that comment/question help Joe deal with his abusive behavior? How could Joe benefit if you were instead to ask how he could avoid choosing abusive responses regardless of his partner's behavior?

Leaders will need to be more directive during the check-in process of early group sessions until group members become familiar with the format and expectations.

FEEDBACK ABOUT TIME OUT

Because the time-out procedure was reviewed in the previous session as one mechanism for avoiding abuse, it is useful to determine to what extent it has been used by group members.

Group leader functions in responding to reports about use of the time-out procedure include the following:

- Monitoring use of time out to determine whether it is used appropriately.
- Reinforcing appropriate use of time out to avoid abusiveness.
- Discouraging inappropriate use of time out such as an excuse to avoid an unpleasant but not critical situation.
- Ensuring the procedure was discussed with the partner.
- Discussing fully abusive incidents in which the time-out procedure was not used but could potentially have averted the abuse.

The review of use of the time-out procedure is not to suggest that there is a quick and easy solution for eliminating men's abusiveness, but rather to emphasize each man's responsibility for doing so. Furthermore, as each man reports to the group, other group members are likely to call him to account for his actions as well as providing support in his attempts to eliminate abuse.

Challenging questions that can be useful when time out has been used inappropriately include the following:

Did your use of time out in that situation serve to protect your partner or yourself?

Challenging questions that are useful as a follow-up to a successful use of time out include the following:

What thoughts about yourself or your partner did you have to overcome to use the time out?

What does your use of time out indicate about your ability to control and direct your actions?

Reviewing time out is useful in reminding group members that they are responsible for and have the ability to eliminate abusive behaviors. This review may be repeated in subsequent sessions if further abusive incidents are disclosed.

ABUSIVE BEHAVIORS

A common frame of reference regarding abuse is a necessary prerequisite to confronting such behavior. Common definitions of abuse are typically limited to examples of physical abuse and intimidation. Although physical abuse has the greatest potential for damage, emotional abuse, domination, and sexual abuse are frequently reported by women to be equally hurtful, especially when they are constant and pervasive. Furthermore, decreases in physical violence in response to legal or social sanctions can be accompanied by increases in other types of abuse. Given the aims of the present program in bringing about comprehensive and enduring change in abusive behavior, a more extensive definition of abuse is required.

Brainstorming Exercise

As a first step in generating a comprehensive definition of abuse, group members are asked to brainstorm, or think up as many examples as they can of abusive behaviors. These examples can then be recorded on a blackboard or flip chart.

Group leader functions during brainstorming include the following:

- Encouraging all members to provide some examples. Calling on less active members individually to provide an example.
- Listing all examples provided.
- Encouraging discussion about the range of examples.
- Indicating that typical definitions of abusiveness tend to leave out some types. Encouraging group members to expand their definitions.

The brainstorming exercise is concluded by indicating that abusive behaviors can be categorized in various ways. One way of categorizing them is provided in Handout 7 (distribute Handout 7).

The representation of abusive behaviors on this handout is likely to generate several types of discussion. Many men will note examples of their partner's behaviors that are depicted in the handout. This discussion, as any discussion of the partner's actions, needs to be challenged by asking how categorizing the partner's behavior assists the man in dealing with his abusiveness.

Emphasis on consequences of particular behaviors can be useful in discussing the definition of abuse. If the consequence of the behavior is hurtful to the partner, then it can be considered abusive. Accepting their partners' perspectives as the definition of abuse is difficult for many men. Fear that the partner will use such a definition to manipulate and control them is frequently voiced. The following challenging questions can be used as responses to such concerns:

> If you disregard your partner when she tells you that what you are doing is painful or upsetting, how will you know what to change in order to stop being abusive?
>
> If believing her means that she has control, I wonder how you would go about establishing a respectful and equal relationship?

To increase each man's awareness of the extent of his abusiveness, each group member can be asked to list his own abusive actions in each of the categories provided. Group members can be asked to indicate which category they regard as the one they most need to change. Pointing out the commonalities can be a way of developing the agenda for future sessions as well as a sense of commonality of purpose or group cohesiveness.

DEFINITIONS OF ABUSIVE AND RESPECTFUL BEHAVIORS

(Distribute Handout 8.) A summary definition of abusive behaviors and the contrasting definition of respectful behaviors are provided in Handout 8. Disregarding and devaluing the partner are central to the definition of abuse. Regarding the partner as equal and autonomous is central to the definition of respect.

These definitions of abuse and respect provide the foundation of the group program. Each group member is encouraged to use these definitions to gauge his own movement from abusive to respectful behavior.

DISTRIBUTE REFLECTIONS LOGS

CHECK-OUT

Session 3: Self-Monitoring

❏ **Goals**

- Define abusive behavior as a choice.
- Develop responsibility for choosing abusive or respectful behaviors.
- Teach self-monitoring as a method of making better choices.
- Introduce the notion that thoughts or beliefs influence actions.

❏ **Outline**

Collect reflections logs
Check-in
Self-monitoring: Handout 9
Role Play 1
Debrief role play
Distribute reflections logs: Handout 5
Check-out

❑ Detailed Agenda for Session 3

COLLECT REFLECTIONS LOGS

CHECK-IN

Reports of failure to use time out and resultant abusiveness or inappropriate use of time-out procedures indicate that this procedure should be reviewed. Leaders, in reviewing time out, may need to emphasize the paramount goal of securing the partner's safety.

Self-monitoring is a process of becoming aware of early warning signals.

SELF-MONITORING

To confront the belief held by many abusive men that their abusive behavior is not within their control, the concept of self-monitoring is introduced. Self-monitoring is a process of becoming aware of early warning signals that precede abusive behavior. These signals include thoughts, bodily reactions, and behavioral indicators. Becoming aware of these signals is described as the first step in making more informed behavioral choices.

Group leaders provide their own examples of early warning signals such as flushing, noting their voice getting louder, sweaty hands, and so on to begin the group discussion.

Brainstorming Exercise

Group members are asked to generate examples of their thoughts, bodily reactions, and behavioral indicators that precede their abusive actions. This is useful in assisting men to note and describe their own signals as well as to become aware of additional signals identified by other group members. Group members can be encouraged to think back to a recent abusive incident and recollect the thoughts and reactions that preceded their abusive behavior.

Group leader functions during brainstorming include the following:

- Identifying some of their own early warning signals to provide examples for the group.
- Encouraging group members to identify their own signals.
- Noting examples from group on a blackboard or flip chart.
- Promoting common identification of signals between group members.

To conclude the brainstorming exercise, a summary of common signals is provided in Handout 9 (distribute Handout 9).

Group leaders can use this handout in the following ways:

- Encourage group members to identify their most common signal in each category.
- Emphasize the category of *thoughts* as a way of introducing beliefs and their connection with bodily reactions and behaviors.
- Encourage discussion about signals by asking group members what alternate behavioral choices they could make in response to particular signals.

Role Play 1

As another way of becoming sensitive to early warning signals, a role play is introduced as an opportunity to observe signals in another person. The male group leader enacts the role of an abusive husband, and the female leader plays the part of his wife. The enactment should be as dramatic as possible and the male leader should attempt to display a range of signals.

Group members can be asked to note signals evidenced by the male leader. Group members are also asked to note their own reactions as they observe the role play.

Scenario. Husband has been home with two sick children while his wife is shopping. Wife has been absent for several hours. She reports on returning that she met a friend who was upset and needed comforting. Husband becomes irate and abusive—yelling, blaming, name-calling. Wife attempts to be conciliatory and explain her actions.

Sample Dialogue

He (loudly) Where have you been? What took you so long?

She I ran into Barbara and she was really upset . . .

He (interrupting) She was upset! What about me? I've been going crazy here with the kids being sick. You should have been home hours ago!

She Well, I knew that you could manage with the kids and Barbara really needed someone to talk to.

He Your kids need you! I needed you here! You're some mother, ignoring your sick kids! I should report you to the child welfare people. You're incompetent and heartless, . . . (continues name-calling, etc.).

Debrief. The aim of debriefing this role play is for each group member to increase his awareness of his own signals.

Questions to guide the discussion can include the following:

What reactions in the husband did you observe that were similar to ones that you have experienced?

What thoughts were probably going through the husband's head as he waited for his wife? Have you had similar thoughts? Did your thoughts lead to abusiveness?

If the husband had been aware of his early warning signals, what alternate behavioral choices could he have made?

The role play also serves the additional purpose of increasing awareness of the consequences of abuse on the partner. Some of the men may voluntarily note that the wife's reactions caused them to feel uncomfortable. The female leader can further encourage this by describing her own reactions to the abuse—for example, fear, hurt, and mistrust. The male group leader can challenge the men to become more aware of and empathize with their partners' reactions. The following is an example of a question that fosters such empathy:

If you paid attention to your partner's reactions in the same way as you noted Mary's reactions, how would that affect your behavior?

It can be noted that a significant deterrent to abuse is an appreciation of the hurt it causes.

In concluding the discussion on self-monitoring, leaders can emphasize the need for regular practice. It can also be noted that as men become more proficient in avoiding abuse, their partners may feel increasingly safe to voice criticisms or distress that up to this time had been suppressed because of fear. This can be defined as a positive change in the relationship and an additional challenge for men to practice self-monitoring as a way of avoiding abusive responses to their partners.

DISTRIBUTE REFLECTIONS LOGS

CHECK-OUT

9

Confronting Abusive Beliefs: Sessions 4, 5, 6, and 7

The stage has been set and the process of belief confrontation can now begin. This is the focus for Sessions 4, 5, 6, and 7.

Allusions to belief systems were present in the first phase of the group process, but direct confrontation of beliefs begins in this phase. In promoting confrontation of abusive beliefs, it is assumed that a common definition of abuse has been accepted by group members, that there is a willingness to examine the connection between beliefs and actions, and that a sufficient degree of group cohesion has been developed so that individuals feel comfortable with self-exploration in the group context.

The aims of this phase are the definition of the concept of beliefs and the understanding that beliefs can lead to abusive actions. Understanding the connection between beliefs and emotional responses is promoted as group members are encouraged to examine the ways in which their emotional responses are shaped by their beliefs. Abusive men's beliefs in the central self, the superior self, and the deserving self are examined to determine how these support abuse. And finally, consequences of abuse are considered to further the process of confronting abusive beliefs.

This phase, therefore, focuses on each man's belief system and the ways in which it supports his abuse. Understanding the nature of these beliefs is necessary because behavior change is unlikely without corresponding belief systems change.

Session 4: Monitoring Beliefs

❑ **Goals**

- Development of an understanding of beliefs and their connection with abusive behavior.
- Identification of personal beliefs that support abusive behavior.

❑ **Outline**

Collect reflections logs
Check-in
Definition of beliefs: Handout 10
Role Play 2
Debrief role play
Distribute reflections logs: Handout 5
Check-out

❑ **Detailed Agenda for Session 4**

COLLECT REFLECTIONS LOGS

CHECK-IN

DEFINITION OF BELIEFS

(Distribute Handout 10.) To provide an understanding of the connection between beliefs and abusive behaviors, a common definition of beliefs is required.

Beliefs can be defined as an individual's ideas about ideal traits and behaviors, about causation, and about end states of existence. The connection between thoughts and beliefs can be clarified by indicating that when one is thinking about something, one can be considered to be reviewing one's beliefs about that topic. For example, in self-monitoring thoughts, particularly those that include "should" or "ought," one is in fact reviewing beliefs about desirable outcomes. These can in some circumstances lead to abusive behaviors.

Beliefs are frequently not consciously considered. Actions may be based on beliefs without awareness of the belief. For example, criticizing a female partner's appearance may be based on the belief that beautiful women enhance the status of the accompanying male. This belief regarding women's appearance, however, may not be one of which the man is consciously aware, even as he feels dissatisfied with his partner's appearance or as he belittles her appearance.

Actions and feelings often provide clues about beliefs. Because actions and expressions of feelings are often based on beliefs, examination of the thoughts that accompany these actions and feelings can indicate what beliefs are held. For example, a man who insists on sexual relations with his partner even when she indicates that she is not interested is likely acting on a belief that as her husband he is entitled to sex whenever he so desires.

Beliefs are often accepted as true without critical examination.

Beliefs are often accepted as true without critical examination. The judgments implicit in beliefs frequently are simply accepted and not questioned. Beliefs about women's inferiority, for example, are widely accepted even in the face of contrary evidence, largely because they are not subject to evaluation.

Self-monitoring thoughts bring beliefs to awareness. The process of consciously considering one's thoughts, particularly in moments preceding abusive actions, increases awareness and understanding of one's own belief system.

Brainstorming Exercise

Generating a list of thoughts that group members experienced before or during a recent abusive incident is a useful way to begin bringing beliefs to awareness. Group members may need to be encouraged to engage in this exercise because they expect to have their beliefs criticized. Group leaders can note that the most effective critical examination of beliefs is that which is done by each man regarding his own beliefs.

Group leader functions during brainstorming include the following:

- Encouraging each member to contribute to the list of thoughts.
- Noting the thoughts on a flip chart or blackboard.
- Noting common beliefs evident such as the centrality, superiority, and deservedness of the self.
- Beginning confronting beliefs through the use of challenging questions such as those listed below.
- Staging interactions between the leaders to demonstrate how judgments are frequently based on beliefs rather than facts—for example, discussion of whether the room is too hot or too cold or whether the lights are too bright or too dim. Demonstrating that each judgment reflects a valid experience defuses any argument about who is "right."
- Encouraging group members to continuously monitor their thoughts and critically examine their beliefs.

Challenging questions that are useful when abusive men insist that they are right in a dispute with their partners include the following:

Which one of you in your relationship determines what is right or wrong?
On what basis is this authority to make judgments made in your relationship?
How does your belief that you are invariably right affect your partner? How does it affect your behavior toward her?

Identification of beliefs is further explored in the following role play.

Role Play 2

The goal in this role play is to have group members identify the actions and reactions of the husband and to begin to speculate about the beliefs that may support these. Also, group members can begin through identification with the husband to understand how their beliefs lead to their own abusive behavior.

Scenario. Husband and wife are discussing their budget. Husband complains of the continual need for car repairs and indicates that he intends to go out and buy a new car. Wife objects, citing other expenses such as children's clothing that have priority. She suggests that they continue to repair the car for the time being. Husband belittles her understanding of cars, blames the wife for all their financial problems, and becomes increasingly abusive while the wife becomes increasingly quiet.

Sample Dialogue

He I had to take the car to the garage again. The transmission needs overhauling and it's going to cost mega bucks. I'm going to trade the old clunker in on a new model instead.

She I'm not sure we can afford that right now. The kids need new clothes for school and a lot of dental work.

He (interrupting) Don't be stupid! If I don't have a car I don't go to work. Then we won't be able to pay for food or rent to say nothing of clothes and dentists.

She Why don't we fix the old car until we're in a better financial position?

He (angrily) You are such a dimwit! You know nothing about cars! Spending on this car is pouring money down the drain. Our finances are a mess because you just throw money away. You are such an irresponsible airhead . . . (continues abusively).

Debrief. The purpose of this debriefing is to promote group members' ability to identify the husband's abusive thoughts and actions, to begin to identify abusive beliefs, and to recognize ways in which such beliefs are reflected in behavior.

Typical responses by group members to the role play include affirmation of the husband's expertise in automotive matters and agreement that the wife's opinion (and women's opinions, generally) are of little relevance. Group leaders, therefore, need to redirect attention to the manner in which the wife's opinions were disregarded in the role play, what this might indicate about the husband's beliefs, how these beliefs allowed the husband to become abusive, and how such beliefs are shared by group members.

Challenging questions that can be used for this purpose include the following:

> How did the husband's beliefs about his place in the family permit him to behave abusively?
>
> How did the husband's beliefs prevent him from listening to his partner and taking her concerns into account?

Self-evaluation can be encouraged by having group members remember similar incidents in their own experiences and asking them to identify the beliefs they were acting on in those situations. The following challenging question can be posed:

> When your partner disagrees with you and you get angry, what kinds of thoughts are behind that anger?

Consideration of alternate belief systems can be useful in encouraging the identification of respectful beliefs. A challenging question of this nature follows:

> What different belief about that situation would help to avoid abusiveness?

Typical responses from group members at this point generally indicate that they are only reluctantly beginning the process of self-evaluation. Encouragement and hope, therefore, need to be provided to affirm that the outcome of the process will be beneficial.

DISTRIBUTE REFLECTIONS LOGS

CHECK-OUT

Session 5: Feelings as Reflecting Beliefs

❏ Goals

- Increase awareness of feelings as arising from beliefs about the self.
- Identify individual beliefs, the feelings they engender, and the acts that follow.

❏ Outline

Collect reflections logs
Check-in
Beliefs about feelings: Handout 11
Role Play 3
Debrief role play
Distribute reflections logs: Handout 5
Check-out

❏ Detailed Agenda for Session 5

COLLECT REFLECTIONS LOGS

CHECK-IN

FEELINGS AS REFLECTING BELIEFS

Male emotional expressiveness is generally viewed as restricted, and therapeutic approaches have been devised to overcome this deficiency (Moore & Haverkamp, 1989). In the present program, however, the problem is defined as one not of behavioral deficit, but rather as an indication of beliefs men hold regarding the appropriate manner and situation for expressing emotions. Specifically, emotional expressiveness in abusive relationships is linked to a belief in the central, superior, and deserving self.

A belief in the central self promotes disregard of the effects of demeaning emotional expressiveness and prevents development of empathy with the partner. A belief in the superior self promotes negative defensive emotional reactions when threats to male superiority are perceived. A belief in the deserving self promotes negative emotional reactions when the partner is perceived to be failing in providing the expected level of care and nurturance.

Anger, as an expressed emotion, is consistent with cultural norms regarding male centrality, superiority, and dominance. It has been suggested that men, therefore, can use anger as a way of controlling their partners and justifying their abusiveness (Campbell, 1991).

Understanding that anger may represent a reaction to culturally prescribed masculine beliefs provides a framework for beginning a process of reevaluation. When results indicate that held beliefs are inconsistent with respectful relationships, then belief change coupled with an expanded range of emotional expressiveness becomes possible.

Brainstorming Exercise

To increase group members' awareness of the connection between beliefs, feelings, and actions, a brainstorming exercise can be used. Group members are instructed to recall an incident involving their partners during which they felt distressed or upset. Group members are asked to generate a list of emotions that they experienced. The emotions elicited are listed on a flip chart or blackboard. Group members are then asked to recall the thoughts that accompanied these feelings. The thoughts and feelings generated are linked to beliefs about themselves and their place in the relationship. Group members are asked to identify how these can lead to abuse.

Typical responses include feelings such as "frustration," "getting pissed off," and "mad." When asked to indicate the thoughts that accompanied such feelings, responses tend to demonstrate expectations that partners should be compliant and subservient. The angry emotion and abusive behavior, therefore, can be linked to lack of compliance with or active challenge of such expectations. Challenging questions that can be used to elicit this connection between emotions, beliefs, and abusive actions include the following:

> Was your feeling of anger related to your belief that your partner had no right to question your authority?
>
> To what extent do your thoughts that you were betrayed and your feelings of anger relate to your belief that you should always come first with your partner?
>
> When you define your emotional distress as anger (rather than fear or confusion or some other feeling), how does that permit you to behave abusively?

Identification of beliefs mediating expression of emotions can be further explored through a role play.

Role Play 3

Group members are instructed to observe and identify the emotions expressed by the husband in this role play. The extent to which these emotions are indications of his beliefs about the relationship can be discussed.

Scenario. Wife has gone back to school and is spending most of her time attending classes and studying. Husband has become responsible for shopping, cooking, cleaning, and child care. Wife rides to school with classmate, George, with whom she also studies. Husband becomes upset with his responsibilities, his wife's lack of concern for him, and her involvement with George. Wife counters that the decision that she resume her schooling was a mutual one that will benefit the family in the long run. Husband escalates conflict by accusing her of being selfish, uncaring, and so on.

Sample Dialogue

He Since you've gone back to school our family has started falling apart. I can't do everything around here while you just hide behind your books or "study" (sarcastically) with George.

She We both agreed that I should go back to school. This is only temporary, and it's hard on me too, you know.

He (angrily) We didn't agree that it was all right for you to be selfish, to ignore your family, and to neglect your kids! And sitting around drinking coffee with George hardly compares with all the work I do around here.

She I'm not being neglectful! I just have a lot of pressure, with assignments . . .

He (interrupting) And I don't have pressure? My job is hell, the kids are wild—I deserve some peace and quiet when I get home, but my uppity wife is too inconsiderate, too involved in her "studies," too self-centered to care about anyone else.

Debrief. The aim of debriefing is to have group members identify the emotions expressed by the husband and to identify his beliefs about his place in the relationship, his relative importance as compared to his wife, and what he believes he deserves from her. Group members are asked to consider how these beliefs influence his emotional and behavioral expressions.

Group members can further be instructed to speculate about emotions that were not expressed and how expression of these suppressed emotions might have led to different behavioral outcomes.

Typical responses from group members include considerable empathy for and identification with the husband's angry responses. The common belief expressed tends to be that the husband's needs are being assigned a lesser priority and this is an understandable reason for anger. Challenging questions that promote reevaluation of the preeminent status of the husband as well as the accompanying anger include the following:

> What kinds of beliefs about his own importance and his place in this relationship are suggested in his angry responses?
>
> If the husband believed his wife to be equally deserving of his help and respect, what emotions might he express? How might his behavior be different?

As men begin to articulate the thoughts and beliefs that underlie particular expressions of emotion, they can be encouraged to reevaluate these beliefs.

(Distribute Handout 11.) The purpose of Handout 11 is to summarize the discussion regarding the links between beliefs, emotions, and actions. Because emotional reactions frequently provide clues to beliefs, attending to the thinking that precedes and accompanies such reactions is important.

Belief reevaluation can incur emotions that are not always experienced as pleasing. For example, periods of confusion and lack of certainty may ensue. If group members are forewarned that such reactions are to be expected, the negative effect can be decreased. These periods of confusion and uncertainty, furthermore, can be redefined as evidence of personal change and growth.

DISTRIBUTE REFLECTIONS LOGS

CHECK-OUT

Session 6: Beliefs About Relationships

❏ Goals

- Increase awareness of beliefs in relationships that support abusive behavior.
- Identification of own beliefs and their effect on one's own abusiveness.

❏ Outline

Collect reflections logs
Check-in
Relationship beliefs
Abusive relationship beliefs: Handout 12
Respectful relationship beliefs: Handout 13
Distribute reflections logs: Handout 5
Check-out

❏ Detailed Agenda for Session 6

COLLECT REFLECTIONS LOGS

CHECK-IN

RELATIONSHIP BELIEFS

The aim of the presentation regarding relationship beliefs is for group members to focus on beliefs about themselves that influence their relationships. It can be suggested that beliefs about the centrality and separateness of the self, the superiority of the self in relation to the partner, and the deservedness of the self can be defined as abusive in that they can lead to abusive actions. In contrast, beliefs in connectedness, equality, and mutual engagement in relationships can be defined as respectful in that they promote respectful relations.

ABUSIVE RELATIONSHIP BELIEFS

Abusive relationship beliefs are generally reflected in men's thoughts before or during abusive incidents. These thoughts typically involve thinking only about the self and disregarding the partner, becoming defensive in relation to perceived threats to superiority or dominance in the relationship, or being outraged that expected service from the partner was not obtained.

An example of a thought that considers only the self and indicates a belief in the central self is "I am unhappy and justifiably angry . . . not abusive." An example of a thought that indicates a belief in the superior self is "I am more rational and, therefore, she should accept my opinion (and not have a different one of her own)." An example of a thought that indicates a belief in the deserving self is "When I come home from a hard day at work, I don't want to hear about her problems with the kids. I want her to listen to me."

Brainstorming Exercise

Group members can begin to identify their abusive beliefs through a brainstorming exercise. Group members are asked to recall a recent abusive incident and focus on the thoughts that were going through their minds at the time. Group leaders encourage each member to identify at least one thought. Some group members may respond that their abusive actions were "automatic" or that they are not aware of any thoughts accompanying their abuse. These group members can be encouraged to practice the self-monitoring techniques presented earlier to increase awareness.

All thoughts elicited are listed on a flip chart or blackboard. Group leaders then can ask group members to identify the beliefs represented by the listed thoughts and encourage discussion about these. The resultant discussion is likely to be lively because association of thoughts with abusive beliefs is likely to generate considerable resistance.

Typical reactions include arguments about the "rationality" of men's thoughts as opposed to the "irrationality" or "unreasonableness" of their partners' behaviors. Closer examination of these examples of "rational" thought, however, generally indicate that they fail to take into account the consequences of men's actions and/or indicate a belief in the generally dominant position of the male. Challenging questions that can be used to elicit such underlying beliefs include the following:

When you don't consider the effect of your actions on your partner, what belief are you acting on?

When you became abusive because she didn't obey you, what belief were you acting on?

How is it that your partner has the responsibility for ensuring that you don't get upset (don't feel bad)?

How does your belief that you are more intelligent and rational permit you to act abusively?

What are the consequences to your relationship of considering that your feelings are more important than hers?

(Distribute Handout 12.) A summary of typical relationship beliefs that can lead to abusive behaviors is provided in Handout 12. Group members are instructed to identify a category that represents thoughts they frequently experience in their interactions with their partners. Group members are asked to consider how these thoughts indicate the beliefs they have about themselves in their relationships and how they can lead to abuse.

RESPECTFUL RELATIONSHIP BELIEFS

As a contrast to abusive beliefs, the following respectful relationship beliefs are provided: the self as connected and concerned about consequences; the self as equal with and seeking collaboration with the partner; the self as mutually and reciprocally engaged in providing care and respect.

(Distribute Handout 13.) Handout 13 provides a summary of respectful relationship beliefs. Leaders may need to explain that respectful beliefs are frequently held concurrently with abusive beliefs. Group members are then asked to identify those respectful beliefs that they hold all the time as well as those to which they sometimes subscribe. It can be pointed out that respectful beliefs are sometimes in conflict with abusive beliefs. Avoiding abuse involves choosing to act on the respectful belief.

Group members are asked to identify one category that requires attention and to report back the following week the extent to which they were able to act on that belief.

DISTRIBUTE REFLECTIONS LOGS

CHECK-OUT

Session 7: Consequences of Abusive Beliefs

❑ Goals

- Focus on the *effects* of abusive behavior.
- Confront the belief in the central self and separate self.
- Have each man consider the effects of his actions on his partner and develop empathy for her experience.

❑ Outline

Collect reflections logs
Check-in
Consequences of abusive actions
Guided reflections
Debrief guided imagery exercise
Consequences of abusive beliefs: Handout 14
Distribute reflections logs: Handout 5
Check-out

❑ Detailed Agenda for Session 7

COLLECT REFLECTIONS LOGS

CHECK-IN

CONSEQUENCES OF ABUSIVE ACTIONS

Focusing abusive men's attention on the consequences of their actions counters their tendency to disregard these consequences and challenges the belief in the central and separate self.

Empathy, or the ability to "stand in the other person's shoes," is developed through focusing on consequences. As abusive men become aware of the fear in their partner's eyes, or begin to appreciate the significance of a flinching gesture in re-

Considering the consequences of abusive acts is likely to be resisted.

sponse to his sudden movement, they begin to connect with her in a way that inhibits further abuse.

Considering the consequences of abusive acts is painful and, therefore, likely to be resisted. It may be necessary to emphasize that one of the most effective ways of stopping abuse is to be fully aware of the outcomes of such actions.

Guided reflections can be used to aid the process of recollecting and appreciating consequences.

GUIDED REFLECTIONS

The group leader describes the process of guided reflections and instructs group members as follows:

> Sit back in your chairs, breathe deeply, and relax all the muscles in your body.
> Think back to the most recent incident in which you were abusive toward your partner.
> Remember the place—what it looked like, who was present.
> Remember what your partner was doing before you were abusive, what the expression on her face was.
> What did you do that was abusive?
> How did she react?
> How did her expression change?
> How was she feeling?
> What was she thinking?
> Try to stay with her feelings, experience those feelings yourself.
> Focus on those feelings.
> Slowly return your thoughts to this room, right now, but keep the memory of your partner's feelings with you.

Debrief. Group leaders need to indicate their appreciation of the sobering nature of this exercise. It can also be useful to note that men are typically discouraged from dwelling on the consequences of their abusive acts, and, therefore, this experience is likely one that was particularly difficult.

Benefits of fully being aware of the outcomes should be reiterated, namely, that such understanding decreases the likelihood of abuse recurring. Also, understanding the effects of their actions on their partners can lead to increased connection with the partner.

However, men also need to be forewarned of potential limitations in the development of connection. Their abuse may have destroyed their partner's trust to such a degree that establishment of connection may not be possible. Unrealistic expectations regarding the salvaging of relationships must be avoided.

CONSEQUENCES OF ABUSIVE BELIEFS

(Distribute Handout 14.) Having considered the consequences of abusive actions, it is also necessary to consider the consequences of beliefs that support such actions. Expectation of the partner's subordination, submission, and caretaking arise from beliefs in the central, superior, and deserving self. These beliefs can have abusive consequences for partners.

Each man is asked to consider the abusive consequences to his partner in each category listed in Handout 14.

Leaders can reiterate that as men's beliefs change, so will their actions and the attendant consequences.

DISTRIBUTE REFLECTIONS LOGS

CHECK-OUT

10

*Developing Respectful Beliefs:
Sessions 8, 9, and 10*

This third phase of the group process aims to begin the process of developing respectful relationship beliefs. Given that belief change is an arduous process and that abusive beliefs are frequently deeply entrenched, the development of respectful beliefs can only be initiated in the course of the present program. Respectful beliefs, therefore, are presented as a desirable goal of the change process, and motivation to continue pursuit of this goal is provided.

A belief in connectedness is promoted through focusing on the ways in which abusive men attend to their partners, and respectful listening is modeled and reinforced.

A belief in relationship equality is fostered through exploring men's disagreements with their partners and the ways in which these are resolved. Mutual engagement is encouraged by having men consider the benefits of increased openness to their partners' perspectives and how this provides opportunities for their own development.

In summary, the aim of this phase of the program is to reinforce respectful beliefs and actions, replacing previous abusive ones. Respectful beliefs are linked with behaviors such as listening, disagreeing, and making choices. The desired direction of change is indicated, and group members are reinforced for movement toward those goals.

The group process typically will require less structure during this phase. A fair degree of group cohesiveness will generally have developed and group members will be interested in each other and confront each other's behavior. Group leaders, however, will still need to point out subtle and pervasive ways in which abusive beliefs continue to influence actions and present barriers to change.

Considerable flexibility in presenting the designated content is desirable. Pursuit of particular issues raised by group members frequently take priority and may provide opportunities for introducing content. Session outlines, therefore, are presented as guides, in the expectation that the order of actual presentation will vary considerably from group to group.

Session 8: Beliefs About Connection

❏ Goals

- Examine beliefs about connection and listening behavior.
- Confront disconnection through disrespectful listening.
- Promote connection through respectful listening.

❏ Outline

Collect reflections logs
Check-in
Beliefs about connection
Disconnecting through disrespectful listening: Handout 15

Connecting through respectful listening: Handout 16
Distribute reflections logs: Handout 5
Check-out

❏ Detailed Agenda for Session 8

COLLECT REFLECTIONS LOGS

CHECK-IN

BELIEFS ABOUT CONNECTION

Belief in the central self supports behavior that disregards or trivializes the other. Abuse is, therefore, likely to occur, because without connection there is no empathy or appreciation of negative effects of one's behavior on the other. Disconnection is characterized by statements and actions that do not consider the effects of these on the partner. Failure to listen to the partner or to take her statements seriously can also indicate disconnection.

Respectful listening demonstrates and fosters connection.

In contrast, a belief in the connected self values connection with the other, places a high regard on the thoughts and feelings of the other, and supports behaviors that aim to strengthen this connection. Respectful listening demonstrates and fosters connection.

DISCONNECTED AND
DISRESPECTFUL LISTENING

The way in which a man listens to his partner provides an indication of his beliefs regarding connection. A belief in the central self, which devalues connection, supports a variety of behaviors that interfere with respectful listening. These listening patterns prevent men from understanding or empathizing with their partners and, therefore, in turn can foster subsequent abusive actions. Failure to hear what they have to say is often experienced as abusive by partners.

Abusive men typically are able to identify distracting behaviors in which they engage while their partners are speaking. These are frequently described as "tuning her out," thinking about other things, or responding with an automatic "uh-huh." The words used to describe a partner's speech, such as "yattering," "nagging," and "squawking," also provide an indication of the belief system that supports disconnection. To heighten awareness of such behaviors, it is useful for group members to identify a range of behaviors that convey lack of respect for the partner while she is speaking.

Brainstorming Exercise

The purpose of this exercise is to develop a list of behaviors that act as barriers to respectful listening. These are identified as blocks to the development of connectedness in a relationship. Connectedness relies on understanding the partner, and this is not possible without first listening and appreciating what she has to say.

Group leader functions during brainstorming include the following:

- Encouraging each group member to identify the ways in which he conveys disrespect for his partner while she is attempting to communicate with him.
- Listing responses on a flip chart or blackboard.
- Promoting discussion regarding the beliefs indicated by these behaviors.
- Emphasizing that such behaviors prevent development of connectedness with their partners.
- Suggesting that a belief in the connected self requires replacing these behaviors with respectful behaviors.

Men can typically identify their dismissive behaviors but are not always prepared to change their belief that these behaviors are acceptable. Challenging questions that can be used to promote such change include the following:

By not listening to your partner, what important information about improving the relationship might you be missing?

(Distribute Handout 15.) Handout 15 presents a way of summarizing disconnecting, disrespectful behaviors. Each group member is instructed to identify a behavior that he uses frequently and is encouraged to notice and change that behavior during the forthcoming week.

CONNECTING THROUGH RESPECTFUL LISTENING

(Distribute Handout 16.) Handout 16 summarizes the relationship between connectedness in a relationship and respectful listening. Respectful listening is described as a way of increasing understanding and connection with the partner. Beliefs about the partner that promote connection are identified. Distinctions between advice giving, problem solving, arguing, agreeing, and listening are highlighted.

This handout can be used as a reminder regarding the importance of connection and the means to achieve it.

The following challenging questions can be posed to encourage men to consider more respectful ways of listening:

> What can you do to change the ways in which you listen to your partner to be more respectful?
>
> How can you demonstrate to your partner that you value connection with her?

Group members may need to be reminded at this point that although they are anxious to demonstrate the ways in which they have changed, their partners may still be fearful of further abuse. Their partners may not be ready to interact in ways they desire, and it is incumbent on them to respect their partners' wishes. A positive approach to dealing with such situations can be promoted through questions such as the following:

> If your partner is not ready to reciprocate your interest in connection, how can you demonstrate that you respect her wishes?

DISTRIBUTE REFLECTIONS LOGS

CHECK-OUT

Session 9: Beliefs About Equality

❏ Goals

- Increase awareness of the effect of a belief in superiority on disagreements.
- Increase awareness of the effect of a belief in equality on disagreements.
- Promote development of belief in equality.
- Promote interactive behaviors based on equality to resolve disagreements.

❏ Outline

Collect reflections logs
Check-in
Beliefs about superiority and disagreement: Handout 17
Beliefs about equality and disagreement: Handout 18
Distribute reflections logs: Handout 5
Check-out

❏ Detailed Agenda for Session 9

COLLECT REFLECTIONS LOGS

CHECK-IN

THE SUPERIOR SELF AND DISAGREEMENT

Abusive men tend not to regard disagreement as a normal part of relationships but rather as a threat to their superiority and dominance. A typical reaction is, therefore, to behave abusively to suppress any evidence of a partner's discontent.

Abusive men's belief in superiority denies their partners the right to their own views and opinions. Notions of duty, loyalty, and love can be used to buttress a man's belief that his opinions should prevail and that his partner's should take second place. Abusive and violent actions are frequently used to reinforce and enforce these beliefs.

Examination of the ways in which a man's belief in superiority and dominance influences his behavior is a necessary precursor to change.

Brainstorming Exercise

Group members are instructed to recall a recent disagreement with their partners. Each man is instructed to recall what kinds of thoughts he had about his partner's right to disagree and about the way in which he thought the disagreement should be resolved. Each man is also asked to identify his behavior that followed from those thoughts or beliefs.

Group leader functions during brainstorming include the following:

- Encouraging each man to recall a disagreement and his thoughts at that time.
- Recording the thoughts on a flip chart or blackboard.
- Identifying the beliefs about himself and his partner that were evidenced in the thoughts about disagreement.
- Identifying any abusive actions that resulted from such beliefs.

Typical responses from group members to this exercise include assertions that their partners should "respect" their opinions or desires. Exploration of this concept of "respect" generally indicates that it is being used synonymously with obedience or acquiescence. Challenging questions that can be used to confront such beliefs include the following:

When you demand "respect" from your partner, how can she indicate that she disagrees with you?

As an adult person, your partner is likely to have views different from yours. How can you show her that it is safe for her to express such views?

(Distribute Handout 17.) Handout 17 summarizes the ways in which a man's belief in superiority prevents resolution of disagreements that are satisfactory to his partner as well as to himself. It is necessary for an abusive man to recognize that in regarding his partner as inferior and by preventing her from having an equal voice in resolving disagreements, he is diminishing the likelihood of establishing a respectful relationship.

Each group member is asked to identify a category that represents thoughts that he frequently experiences.

THE EQUAL SELF AND DISAGREEMENT

A belief in equality in the relationship is evidenced in thoughts and actions that promote mutually satisfying resolution to disagreements. Thoughts that include the naturalness and necessity of open expression of disagreement in a relationship provide evidence of equality beliefs. Different but equal perspectives are validated by men endorsing equality in their relationships.

(Distribute Handout 18.) Handout 18 summarizes beliefs in equality in relationships that are evidenced in disagreements. These beliefs are considered necessary to reach resolutions that are mutually satisfying and hence likely to promote respectful relations.

Each group member is instructed to identify those thoughts that would be helpful in handling disagreements with his partner. Each man is asked to consider how his behavior would be different if he acted on these identified thoughts. Each man can be asked to make a commitment to act on the belief in equality in handling a disagreement during the forthcoming week.

The following challenging questions can be used to promote equality in relationships:

How would letting go of a belief in your superiority over your partner change your behavior during a disagreement?
How could you indicate to her during a disagreement that you regard her as an equal?

DISTRIBUTE REFLECTIONS LOGS

CHECK-OUT

Session 10: Moving Toward Mutuality

❏ **Goals**

- Increase awareness of a belief in deservedness and its effect on the relationship.
- Promote development of a belief in mutual engagement.
- Encourage personal change that is a function of mutual engagement.

❏ **Outline**

Collect reflections logs
Check-in
Beliefs about mutuality
Steps toward mutuality: Handout 19
Distribute reflections logs: Handout 5
Check-out

❏ **Detailed Agenda for Session 10**

COLLECT REFLECTIONS LOGS

CHECK-IN

BELIEFS ABOUT MUTUALITY

Transforming a belief in deservedness in which care and nurturance is unidirectional to a belief in mutual engagement in which the exchange is bidirectional and reciprocal requires a substantial alteration in a man's belief system. This shift presupposes that a connection with the partner exists and that the partner is perceived as having equal rights within the relationship. The shift to mutuality further requires a recognition that the partner not only has equal rights but also has equal needs. Furthermore, mutuality requires a receptivity to the influence of the partner and a recognition that such influence enriches the man's experience and provides him with the opportunity to extend his boundaries and horizons.

Making choices between conflicting alternatives is an area in which beliefs about mutuality can be examined. Abusive men frequently find it particularly difficult to allow their views or choices to be influenced by their partners. Attending to a partner's needs or respecting her views tends to be perceived as male submission rather than as evidence of mutuality.

Redefining a man's actions demonstrating mutual engagement as signs of courage and strength can be used to foster such acts. Redefining relationships and individuals within relationships as continually growing and evolving can counter an abusive man's assertions that "that's the way I am." His partner's efforts to produce change thereby also can be redefined as positive, growth-producing forces.

Restrictive definitions of reciprocity, in which a man asserts that having done something for his partner she is now required to do something for him, need to be confronted. Mutuality does not include demands for service, or unilateral decision making. It requires consideration of the partner's wishes and an openness to be influenced by these wishes.

STEPS TOWARD MUTUALITY

(Distribute Handout 19.) Making choices when faced with conflicting alternatives is an opportunity to examine abusive men's beliefs about deservedness and mutuality. The ability to take the partner's wants and needs into account and to move in a direction that respects her is evidence of a movement toward mutuality. Making the distinction between engagement and submission is particularly difficult for abusive men.

Instructing group members to recall an event in which they were faced with a choice that required them to take their partners into account can be a useful way of demonstrating mutual engagement. Evidence of mutual engagement is growth or change in the man's perspective. He may or may not agree with his partner but he has gained a greater appreciation of her views.

Group members can be encouraged to describe the behaviors that followed from an increased understanding and appreciation of their partners. Evidence of change on the man's part is defined as movement toward mutuality and relationship growth.

Challenging questions that can be used to guide this discussion include the following:

> How can you convey to your partner that you want to understand her point of view and are open to making changes that might result from such understanding?
> How can you ensure that you always take her views into account, even when you find them objectionable?
> What limits your ability to be mutually engaged with your partner? What can you do about it?
> If your partner is not ready to engage with you, what can you do to demonstrate that you respect her wishes?

DISTRIBUTE REFLECTIONS LOGS

CHECK-OUT

11

Consolidating Changed Beliefs: Sessions 11 and 12

The process of changing beliefs in the central, superior, and deserving self to beliefs in the connected, equal, and mutually engaged self is typically only started during the 12-week program. With the aim of consolidating the changes made and promoting an ongoing change process, the last two sessions are devoted to review and charting future directions.

The last two sessions, therefore, have been structured as a review. These sessions provide the opportunity to recognize changes that have been made, frequently through a difficult and uncomfortable process.

Progress made during the program typically consists of a raised level of awareness, an identification of areas requiring change, and expression of desire to continue the process of self-examination and belief change.

Each man in the group will have progressed at his own rate, resulting in a range of changes within the group from the minute to the spectacular. Individual change, no matter how small, is to be recognized and applauded.

Session 11: Beliefs—From Past to Future

❏ **Goals**

- Review changes in beliefs and actions.
- Reinforcement of positive changes made.

❏ **Outline**

Collect reflections logs
Check-in
Beliefs—From past to future: Handout 20
Distribute reflections logs: Handout 5
Check-out

❏ **Detailed Agenda for Session 11**

COLLECT REFLECTIONS LOGS

CHECK-IN

BELIEFS—FROM PAST TO FUTURE

(Distribute Handout 20.) As a process of review, each group member is instructed to consider the changes that he has made in each of the areas addressed by this program. The contrast between old beliefs and new beliefs is to be emphasized as is the link between the new belief and the new behavior that it supports.

As part of the review process, it is important to reinforce positive changes made. In particular, movement from self beliefs reflecting centrality, superiority, and deservedness to beliefs that encompass connectedness, equality, and mutuality deserve recognition and approbation.

Group members need to be forewarned that total and complete replacement of abusive beliefs by respectful beliefs is unlikely, and they can expect to experience recurrent ambivalence and confusion as the process of belief change continues. Furthermore, they may find themselves inclined to act on their abusive beliefs. Group members can be challenged to demonstrate the strength and courage required to continue making respectful behavioral choices.

DISTRIBUTE REFLECTIONS LOGS

CHECK-OUT

Session 12: Review and Feedback

❏ **Goals**

- Evaluation by each group member of his own progress and the progress of every other group member.
- Individual feedback to all group members and leaders by each person present.

❏ **Outline**

Collect reflections logs
Review and feedback: Handout 21

Closing summary

Check-out

❏ Detailed Agenda for Session 12

COLLECT REFLECTIONS LOGS

REVIEW AND FEEDBACK

(Distribute Handout 21.) This final group exercise is introduced as a process in which each group member has an opportunity to reflect on himself as well as to provide feedback to all other group members and to both group leaders.

Each group member is required, as part of the exercise, to describe the changes he has made in his beliefs and behaviors as a result of the group and to identify those that still require change.

Each man, then, in turn addresses each group member present and provides feedback regarding the positive changes that he observed in this person and those areas that require further work.

Group members receiving feedback are asked to listen respectfully without responding or making rebuttal.

Each group member is also asked to provide feedback to group leaders about what was done that was particularly helpful and what was not done that he would have liked.

Group leaders provide feedback in a similar fashion once all group members have had their turn. In this way, they can counter any unduly negative statements that may have been made about individuals during this process. It also helps to ensure that the group ends on a positive note.

CLOSING SUMMARY

Leaders, in closing, can make general observations about the positive changes they have observed. Also, a general acknowledgment of the contributions of the group members to the group process is in order.

CHECK-OUT

The last check-out provides an opportunity for each group member to say a final word and to bid farewell to the group.

PART V

Program Outcomes

12

Program Outcomes

Program outcome can be determined using various indicators. The most widely used indicators have been standardized measures in which men self-report their behavior. Partner's reports are frequently used to supplement these, as women's reports tend to diverge somewhat from that of the men. Standardized measures of various aspects of abusive men's psychological functioning are also frequently used as supplementary indicators of change.

Behavioral and psychological measures, however, are not sufficient to assess changes in beliefs about the self, the partner, and the relationships. Standardized measures of belief systems of abusive men do not exist. Evaluation of change, therefore, must be obtained through intensive interviews with the men in which they describe their current thinking as well as reflect back on their change process.

Evaluation of the present program used both standardized measures and intensive interviews to chart the progress of the men in the program and at follow-up. A summary analysis of both the standardized measures and the narratives of the men on follow-up are presented in this chapter.

❑ **Violence, Psychological**
    Abuse, and Depression

Evaluation of outcome based on standardized measures was obtained for 25 men who completed the program and their 19 partners.
At 3-month follow-up, results were obtained from 13 men and 11
partners. Although the number of cases is relatively small, the convergence of men's self-reports, women's reports, and qualitative
analyses of intensive interviews provides validation that significant
clinical as well as statistical results were obtained.

Assessment of levels of physical abuse were based on the violence
subscale of Straus's (1979) Conflict Tactics Scale (CTS).

Psychological abuse was monitored using Tolman's (1989) Psychological Maltreatment of Women Scale (PMWS). Depression levels were assessed using Hudson's (1982) Generalized Contentment
Scale (GCS). Results were obtained from both men and women on
the first two measures, and for men alone on the depression scale.

Results indicated significant reductions in all measures as reported by both the men and their partners from pre- to postprogram.
At 3-month follow-up, all reductions had not only been maintained
but continued to demonstrate further reductions. Physical violence
had virtually been eliminated at follow-up, with only 1 of the 13 men
reporting any violent behavior. The 11 partners, who consistently
reported higher levels of violence than the men, nevertheless cor-
roborated the significant and continuing decline. Psychological
abuse, which had been dramatically reduced during the program,
continued to decline at follow-up, at least according to the men.
Their partners reported maintenance, but no further reductions.
Men's levels of depression evidenced similar decline, from a level
indicating clinical depression at the beginning of the program to
levels in the normal range at follow-up. Average scores for the men
and their partners are summarized in Table 12.1.

The observation that men's physical as well as psychological abuse
was reduced and that their behavior continued to change during the
follow-up interval provides support for belief systems theory. Specifically, these results support the hypothesis that in bringing about
belief systems change, more enduring and comprehensive changes
in behavior will result. The continued reduction in abuse following

Table 12.1 Violence, Abuse, and Depression Scores as Reported by Men and Their Partners at Preprogram, Postprogram, and Program Follow-Up

Measure	Time		
	Preprogram	*Postprogram*	*Program Follow-Up*
CTS (men's report)	2.8	1.2	0.7
CTS (women's report)	9.5	2.4	1.5
PMWS (men's report)	110.1	90.6	82.5
PMWS (women's report)	163.3	125.9	125.1
GCS (men's report)	39.2	33.6	22.5

NOTE: CTS = Conflict Tactics Scale (Straus, 1979); PMWS = Psychological Maltreatment of Women Scale (Tolman, 1989); GCS = Generalized Contentment Scale (Hudson, 1982).

program completion suggests that the process of belief change, which was admittedly only begun during the program, was one that continued for the men. Additional evidence of this continuing process of belief change was found in the narratives of the men at follow-up.

❏ Movement Toward Respectful Beliefs

Fifteen men were contacted after an interval ranging from 3 to 18 months following program completion. Each man was asked to participate in an interview that involved reflecting back on the program and thinking about changes he had made during and after the program. All interviews were taped and transcribed.

Transcripts were analyzed to determine the extent to which there had been movement from the previously held abusive beliefs in the central, superior, and deserving self toward the beliefs in the connected, equal, and mutually engaged self. Statements were coded using Strauss and Corbin's (1990) grounded theory method.

Results demonstrated that the vast majority of men identified abusive beliefs that had contributed to their abusive behavior, indicated that some change had ensued, and realized that further change was required. Two of the men on follow-up were still reluctant to concede that their beliefs or actions had or required change. These men were particularly entrenched in their belief that they were superior to their partners. The remainder of the men, however, explicitly described changes that they had noted in themselves and frequently added that these changes had also been noted by their partners.

Several men expressed regret that they had not made changes earlier.

Ambivalence about belief change and inconsistency in behaviors were typically reported. Fear was expressed in some instances that changes had been excessive, particularly in the direction of the equal self. The need for further change, however, was generally acknowledged and several men expressed regret that they had not made changes earlier. The changes observed ranged from fairly superficial to profound alterations in perspectives on relationships. Summaries of belief changes are provided below.

THE CONNECTED SELF

Change from belief in the central self to the connected self ranged from the somewhat superficial recognition that the partner is a person who is affected by the man's behavior to a more profound understanding of the pain the man's abuse had caused the partner.

All the men made observations indicating an awareness of the effect of their behavior on the partner. Some of this awareness was at a fairly rudimentary level.

Now I know it's not OK to be abusive to get your own way or to make people feel as awful as you do.

I'm not the centerpiece of the relationship any more.

Other statements indicated the beginnings of empathy, the ability to appreciate the feelings of the partner. This developing empathy frequently led to some moderation of the man's behavior.

I'm being a little more respectful and putting myself in the other person's place.

I try to listen to people and I think, well, they have feelings too!

Now I stop to think, whereas before I would say something and it was abusive. Now I choose my words so they don't offend the other person.

A beginning sense of connectedness was demonstrated in the recognition that a partner was affected by a man's actions and that her feelings were significant and important. Understanding his partner's and children's suffering and appreciating the resultant lack of trust was frequently a profoundly moving experience.

When we're together, I try to be a lot more conscious of her. I see her as a more defined person—she has feelings. She always did, but now these feelings mean a lot more.

I've recognized the effects of the violence. . . . If something was on her mind she couldn't bring it up because she felt maybe I would blow up. . . . I know she doesn't feel safe and the trust is not there toward me.

I can see the damage that I've done to my wife and kids by being emotionally and verbally abusive to them. . . . My wife hides things from me . . . my kids won't tell me things because they're afraid of my reactions.

One man, who had gained an appreciation of connectedness, spoke with considerable sadness about the length of time it took him to make the discovery.

Beginnings of empathy were noted.

Now I know you gotta pay more attention to who is most important in your life. It took a year or so to find out my wife was the most important person in my life and now it's a little too late for that.

In summary, the men interviewed indicated that their belief in the central and separate selves had been dislodged, at least to the extent that there was recognition that their partners had feelings and were affected by the men's abusive behavior. Beginnings of empathy were noted and, in some cases, an appreciation of the value of connectedness. However, there was as yet little expressed desire or curiosity about the partner as a whole complex person, or an appreciation of connection as an enriching and growth-producing experience for the man or for the relationship.

THE EQUAL SELF

Movement from the superior self to the equal self was evidenced by the majority of the men who indicated a newly acquired appreciation of the partner, her opinions, and her contributions to the relationship. In the program, movement toward equality (as well as connection) was promoted through emphasizing that men could benefit by listening to their partners. The belief that the partner was an equal and important person was operationalized, in part, through listening to her in a respectful manner. A change toward valuing the partner and what she had to say was evidenced in the statements of the majority of the men.

> I realize that my wife has some valuable opinions. . . . It's too bad that I didn't stop to listen 5 years ago or I might not have caused all these problems.

> The biggest thing for me is just trying to listen to other people . . . whatever they think—that's their opinion. . . . I don't feel rejected now when others' opinions differ.

> I think that I'm listening better, or maybe it's that I'm realizing that I'm not listening as good as I could.

Although some men indicated a beginning acceptance of the notion of equality, others still could not shake their belief in relationships as hierarchical. These men indicated that although they had altered their behavior in the direction of greater equality, they still harbored a fear that they had given up a one-up position for a one-down position.

> I think that I give in too easy . . . whatever she wanted to do I would do.

> I've taken such a huge step backward . . . leaving everything in her hands. . . . It's like I'm so afraid of screwing up again. . . . Now it's like I almost need to learn to take a bit more back.

The notion of joint decision making or consideration of both perspectives was not fully appreciated by these men who still described interactions in terms of "giving in" and "taking back." The emphasis in male socialization on hierarchical relationships appears to be particularly difficult to overcome for some men.

In summary, movement from the superior self to the equal self was evident in the universal descriptions of changes in listening behavior and appreciation of benefits derived from those changes. Some of the men described genuine valuing of the partner as an equal, at least in some aspects of the relationship. Other men still had difficulty with the notion of equality and of valuing different perspectives in decision making, and they indicated a fear that the superior-inferior equation in the relationship had simply reversed itself. Although the belief in the superior self had been challenged, the replacement of this belief with one in relationships as equal partnerships tended to be more difficult for some men than others.

THE MUTUALLY ENGAGED SELF

Movement toward a belief in the mutually engaged self requires a degree of connection and equality with the partner. Therefore, only modest movement toward mutuality was observed. Confrontation of the belief in the deserving self was only partially successful because men had difficulty in appreciating the extent to which their needs and desires were accommodated by their partners and their families.

> I realize that I've got areas in my life where I have to change. . . . [Before] I was expecting people to change to accommodate to my feelings. . . . Realizing that I have to change is a significant step.

Expectations of being cared for and nurtured by partners were exceedingly difficult for the men to forgo. A number of men indicated that they simply were not prepared to accommodate their partners.

> She said, "Just give me time to learn to trust you," . . . [but] finally one day I said, "Forget it, we're through!" I just wasn't being loved enough!

Developing a belief in the mutually engaged self appears to be beyond the scope of the present program for most men. A recognition was obtained that abuse is not warranted when expectations of deservedness are not met. However, a belief in mutual engagement in which a man changes and is changed through his equal, reciprocal, and respectful interaction with his partner appears to be elusive. Given men's struggles in developing beliefs in the connected and equal selves, it may be that only the desirability of endorsing a belief in the mutually engaged self can be provided in the present program.

❏ Conclusion

Confronting men's abusive beliefs through interactional group therapy has been demonstrated to result in behavior change, psychological change, as well as changes in beliefs that support such behaviors and processes. Both the men and their partners noted that these changed beliefs had resulted in changed behaviors and social interactions.

Changes observed in the belief systems in some cases appear to be limited, particularly when compared to desired outcomes. However, the process of bringing beliefs to awareness, confronting them, and considering alternatives is a continuous process that was initiated during group therapy and potentially will continue after group completion. A more extensive follow-up period would determine to what extent this change continued in the desired direction.

Appendix: Handouts

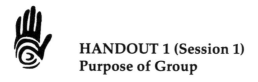

HANDOUT 1 (Session 1)
Purpose of Group

This group program aims to assist men who have been abusive toward their partners to end their abusive behavior. This is done by examining beliefs that support abusive behavior and replacing them with beliefs and behaviors that promote respectful relationships.

The program considers the following questions:

- How do you determine if behavior is abusive?
- Who is responsible for curbing abusiveness? How can this be done?
- How do beliefs about the self and others in relationships lead to abuse?
- What is the process by which beliefs lead to abuse?
- What are the effects of abusive behavior?
- How can you be more connected with your partner?
- How do your beliefs about equality influence your relationships?
- How can you move toward greater mutuality in your relationships?
- How can you prevent future abuse?

HANDOUT 2 (Session 1)
Participant Agreement

I wish to participate in this group with the aim of becoming aware of and eliminating my abusive behavior toward my partner.

I understand that participation in the group involves talking about myself, listening to others, and interacting with others in a helpful manner. Such participation will maximize the usefulness of the group for myself and other members.

I promise to keep in confidence the names and identities of all group members. I understand that the group leaders will respect this confidentiality with certain specific exceptions. These exceptions include legal requirements to report incidents of child abuse and threats against or risks to the safety of others.

If my ability to participate in a group session is impaired by drugs or alcohol, I understand that I may be refused admittance or asked to leave.

I recognize that to receive maximum benefit from the group program I need to attend all sessions and to arrive on time. If I cannot attend a particular session I agree to inform a group leader in advance and to explain my absence at the subsequent group session.

In summary, I agree to

1. Commit myself to eliminating my abusive behavior.
2. Be open to learning how my behavior is abusive.
3. Examine my beliefs that support abusiveness.
4. Use group time to talk about situations that involved abusive thoughts, feelings, and behaviors on my part.
5. Use group time to give feedback to other group members about how their thoughts and/or behaviors affect others.
6. Keep in confidence names and identities of all group members.
7. Attend all group sessions regularly and on time. When I cannot attend I will call _____ at _____ as soon as possible and leave a message.

I agree to all of the above.

Signature _____   Date _____
Witness   _____

145

HANDOUT 3 (Session 1)
Initial Self-Disclosure

1. Describe your abusive behavior that led to your decision to attend this group.

2. How long and in what ways have you been abusive toward your current partner?

3. What effect has your abusive behavior had on your partner? On your children?

4. Have you been abusive with previous partners? In what way(s)?

5. Are you presently living with your partner? What is her name? What are your hopes for the relationship?

6. Do you have children? What are their names? How much contact do you have with them?

7. In what specific ways would you like to see your behavior changed in 6 months' time?

HANDOUT 4 (Session 1)
Time Out

Purpose: To keep your partner safe when you fear you are becoming abusive.

Before the abuse starts you should:

- Discuss the procedure beforehand with your partner.
- Indicate that this is an action you are taking to prevent repeating abusive behavior.
- Discuss beforehand *how long* you will be gone.
- Agree on a signal that you can use, for example, "I'm ready to blow . . . I need a time out."

What to do when you are becoming abusive:

- Leave the situation immediately.
- Stay away the agreed-on length of time.
- Do things that are calming—take deep breaths, walk briskly, and so on.

What not to do:

- Don't drink, do drugs, or drive.
- Don't review the argument in your mind.

When you return:

- Tell your partner you have returned as agreed *and*
- Calmly negotiate a time to discuss the problem *or*
- Repeat the time out.

Remember:

It takes strength and courage to leave a potentially abusive situation. You are not "wimping out."

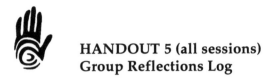

HANDOUT 5 (all sessions)
Group Reflections Log

Session _____

1. What happened in group this week that was particularly relevant to your situation?

2. What did you learn about yourself this week?

3. How would you have liked the session to be different?

HANDOUT 6 (Session 2)
Check-In

Purpose:

- To present *yourself* and your experiences in dealing with your abusive behaviors honestly and openly to the group.
- To listen carefully while others check in, asking questions only for clarification.

Format: Describe an incident during the past week in which you chose abusive behavior or chose to avoid becoming abusive.

> Describe *your* actions, thoughts, and feelings.
> Describe the *effect* of your actions on *others*.

When you check in:

> Remember:
> > The purpose is to examine your thoughts and actions and their effects.
> > Be clear and specific about what you *thought* and *did* and what *effect* these had.
> > This process may be uncomfortable, but it is a necessary step in bringing about change.

HANDOUT 7 (Session 2)
Abusive Behaviors

Physically abusing

Typical examples
- pushing, shoving
- hitting, slapping
- holding down
- showing or
  using weapons

Your examples:
_____
_____
_____
_____

Dominating

Typical examples
- threatening
- destroying objects
- controlling decisions
- controlling money
- limiting partner's
  activities

Your examples:
_____
_____
_____
_____

Demanding service

Typical examples
- requiring partner
  to be caretaker
- requiring partner
  to be comforter
- treating partner
  as servant
- expecting partner
  to look after
  your feelings

Your examples:
_____
_____
_____

Minimizing, blaming

Typical examples
- ignoring abusiveness
- joking about abuse
- blaming abuse
  on others
- blaming abuse
  on partner

Your examples:
_____
_____
_____
_____

Emotionally abusing

Typical examples
- insulting
- name calling, belittling
- discrediting partner's
  opinions

Your examples:
_____
_____
_____
_____

Sexually abusing

Typical examples
- forced sex
- repeated unwanted
  touching
- repeated unwanted
  sexual demands
  or behaviors

Your examples:
_____
_____
_____

 **HANDOUT 8 (Session 2)**
Definitions

Abusive behavior

• Behavior that inflicts hurt or injury through disregard, domination, or inequitable demands of partner. Abusive behaviors include use of physical violence, demeaning language, domination, and demands for service.

Respectful behavior

• Behavior that conveys consideration for the partner as an equal person and connects with the partner in a mutual fashion.

HANDOUT 9 (Session 3)
Self-Monitoring

Early warning signals of your becoming abusive:

Thoughts
"She is always doing this" (Going over past grievances).
"I don't deserve this" (Justifying your abuse).
"I am in charge here" (Needing to be in control).
"She is pushing my buttons" (Not being responsible for own actions).
Your examples:

_____

_____

Body reactions
Muscle tension—for example, tight stomach, shoulders, neck
Pain—for example, head, chest, stomach
Breathing change—for example, faster, shallower
Feeling hot or cold
Shaking
Sweating
Change in skin color—flushing, blanching
Visual distortions—for example, spots, tears, tunnel vision
Your examples:

_____

_____

Behavioral indicators
Agitation, restlessness
Difficulty speaking—for example, dry mouth, stuttering
Getting louder, shriller
Speaking faster or slower
Facial distortions
Clenching hands, making fists
Your examples:

_____

_____

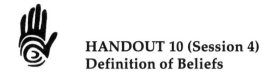

HANDOUT 10 (Session 4)
Definition of Beliefs

Beliefs are an individual's thoughts about ideals, existence, and causation: about how things *should be,* how things *are,* or how things *happen.*

Beliefs are often taken for granted. One may act on a belief without consciously considering the belief.

Beliefs are expressed in thoughts, feelings, and actions. These provide clues to beliefs of which one may not be aware.

Beliefs are ideas held to be true or accepted as self-evident, often without critical examination.

HANDOUT 11 (Session 5)
Feelings as Reflecting Beliefs

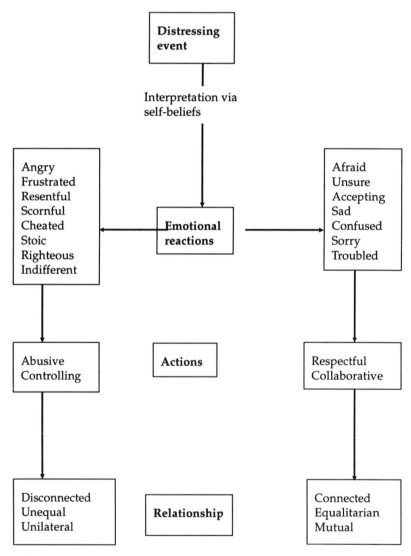

Distressing event

Interpretation via
self-beliefs

| Angry
Frustrated
Resentful
Scornful
Cheated
Stoic
Righteous
Indifferent | ← | **Emotional reactions** | → | Afraid
Unsure
Accepting
Sad
Confused
Sorry
Troubled |

| Abusive
Controlling | **Actions** | Respectful
Collaborative |

| Disconnected
Unequal
Unilateral | **Relationship** | Connected
Equalitarian
Mutual |

154

HANDOUT 12 (Session 6)
Abusive Relationship Beliefs

Abusive relationship beliefs are expectations of or beliefs about the partner that support abusive behaviors.

Obedience

Typical examples:
- she should do what I say
- she should agree with me
- my wishes must prevail
- my will be done

Your examples:
_____
_____
_____
_____

Subordination

Typical examples:
- I am smarter
- I am tougher
- I am more rational
- she is more emotional
- she is never right

Your examples:
_____
_____
_____
_____

Servility

Typical examples:
- I deserve her full attention
- my needs should come first
- attention to other men = unfaithfulness

Your examples:
_____
_____
_____
_____

Blamable

Typical examples:
- she overreacts, is too sensitive
- she started it
- I am not to blame
- she causes problems

Your examples:
_____
_____
_____
_____

Submission

Typical examples:
- only one can be in charge and I am it
- I earn more money so I have more say
- she must not question my judgment

Your examples:
_____
_____
_____
_____

Caretaking

Typical examples:
- she should comfort me
- she should make me feel good
- she shouldn't upset me
- she should meet my sexual needs

Your examples:
_____
_____
_____
_____

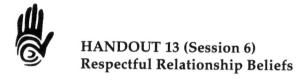

HANDOUT 13 (Session 6)
Respectful Relationship Beliefs

Beliefs about the nature of the relationship between yourself and your partner that promote respect.

Connected but different

Typical examples:
- it is all right to differ
- she has a right to her own opinions
- differences do not mean disloyalty
- having different interests and activities makes us better

Your examples:
_____
_____
_____
_____

Equal

Typical examples:
- I am better in some areas and she is in others
- sharing the load is better than carrying the whole burden alone

Your examples:
_____
_____
_____
_____

Reciprocal

Typical examples:
- we both need to care for each other
- sometimes her needs come before mine
- we respect each other's wishes

Your examples:
_____
_____
_____
_____

Concerned about consequences

Typical examples:
- I am responsible for my actions
- my actions have effects
- effect on her must be considered

Collaborative

Typical examples:
- it is better to make decisions together
- judgment is not dependent on earning
- we do things for each other

Mutual

Typical examples:
- I am as responsible for this relationship as my partner
- I need to understand my partner
- I need to spend time and effort on this relationship

Your examples:

Your examples:

Your examples:

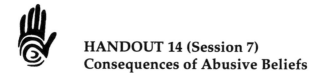

HANDOUT 14 (Session 7)
Consequences of Abusive Beliefs

These beliefs about or expectations of your partner can have abusive consequences. Indicate the abusive consequences your partner has experienced as a result of your adherence to the beliefs below.

Obedience
(expecting her
to obey)

_____
_____
_____
_____
_____
_____
_____
_____

Subordination
(believing her to
be less)

_____
_____
_____
_____
_____
_____
_____
_____

Servility
(expecting service
from her)

_____
_____
_____
_____
_____
_____
_____
_____

Blamable
(blaming her)

_____
_____
_____
_____
_____
_____
_____

Submission
(expecting her to
accept your authority)

_____
_____
_____
_____
_____
_____
_____

Caretaking
(expecting to be
cared for)

_____
_____
_____
_____
_____
_____
_____

HANDOUT 15 (Session 8)
Disconnecting Through Disrespectful Listening

Connection with your partner requires attending and listening to her. *Barriers* to respectful listening are as follows:

Filtering, dreaming

Typical examples:
- hearing only part of what is said
- letting thoughts stray as she talks
- thinking up good responses

Your examples:

_____
_____
_____
_____

Prejudging

Typical examples:
- dismissing emotional statements
- considering partner's judgment irrelevant
- judging partner less experienced

Your examples:

_____
_____
_____

Comparing

Typical examples:
- replacing partner's concerns with yours—for example, I feel abused, I work harder than you

Your examples:

_____
_____
_____

Derailing, placating

Typical examples:
- changing topic
- joking about a serious concern
- ungenuine agreement

Your examples:

_____
_____
_____

Sparring, being right

Typical examples:
- insisting on being right
- put-down of partner
- shouting over partner's voice
- bringing up partner's past

Your examples:

_____
_____
_____

Advising, mind reading

Typical examples:
- giving unsolicited advice
- jumping to conclusions
- telling partner what she *really* thinks

Your examples:

_____
_____
_____

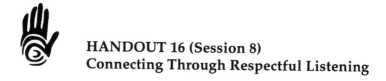

HANDOUT 16 (Session 8)
Connecting Through Respectful Listening

Connection requires respectful listening. *Connecting* through respectful listening results in *increased understanding* of your partner.

Thoughts about your partner that promote connection include:

- My partner's feelings are genuine and valid, and I can benefit from listening to her express them.
- My partner is a unique person and inevitably different from me in some ways.
- My partner is able to solve problems; I don't need to provide solutions.
- My partner has thoughts and ideas that are as good as mine, and sometimes, better than mine.
- My partner's concerns are valid and deserve my full attention.
- My partner's concerns are as important as mine.

Connecting with your partner through respectful listening is easier if you remember:

- Listening means attending to and concentrating on what your partner is saying. It is *not* a passive process.
- Listening will give you valuable information about how your partner is feeling.
- Listening helps you understand your partner's views and how they differ from yours. This is essential in dealing with differences.
- Listening to increase understanding does not include advice giving.
- Listening does not mean taking on responsibility for solving problems.
- Listening does not imply agreement, but does imply taking your partner's concerns seriously.
- Listening indicates a shared concern about issues and promotes mutual actions.
- Arguing is *not* listening.

HANDOUT 17 (Session 9)
Beliefs About Superiority and Disagreement

A belief in one's superiority leads to the following disagreement beliefs that preclude *mutually satisfying* resolutions.

Duty to agree

Typical examples:
- a dutiful partner should agree
- I have the right to my partner's agreement
- I expect my partner to comply

Your examples:
_____
_____
_____
_____

Superiority must prevail

Typical examples:
- being more rational, I am right
- emotionality equals irrationality
- being more experienced, I am right

Your examples:
_____
_____
_____
_____

Disagreement = disloyalty

Typical examples:
- I deserve acquiescence
- not accepting my views is disloyalty
- disagreement leads to unfaithfulness

Your examples:
_____
_____
_____
_____

Disagreement = challenge

Typical examples:
- disagreement equals lack of respect
- disagreement equals blaming
- my partner must not challenge me

Your examples:
_____
_____
_____
_____

Might is right

Typical examples:
- power/money define what is right
- lesser mortals don't have the right to disagree

Your examples:
_____
_____
_____
_____

Love conquers all

Typical examples:
- disagreements can be resolved by sex
- if my partner loved me she would agree

Your examples:
_____
_____
_____
_____

HANDOUT 18 (Session 9)
Beliefs About Equality and Disagreement

Believing in an equal relationship leads to the following disagreement beliefs that promote *mutually satisfying* resolutions.

Disagreements are normal

Typical examples:
- caring partners often disagree
- I cannot expect her to always agree with me
- I cannot demand agreement

Your examples:
_____
_____
_____
_____

Either or neither may be right

Typical examples:
- each person has his or her own point of view
- her ideas may be as good or better than mine
- emotions do not invalidate opinions

Your examples:
_____
_____
_____
_____

Trusting relationships require openness

Typical examples:
- trust is based on accepting differences
- hiding or suppressing differences can lead to mistrust

Your examples:
_____
_____
_____
_____

Disagreements ≠ challenge

Typical examples:
- disagreements can be expressions of concern
- disagreements are not competition
- assumptions about blame and hostile intent may be wrong

Your examples:
_____
_____
_____
_____

Equal and different is OK

Typical examples:
- she is my equal and I respect her differences
- having more money/ strength/experience does not make me right

Your examples:
_____
_____
_____
_____

Love withers when bound

Typical examples:
- loving means freedom to disagree
- sex doesn't resolve differences

Your examples:
_____
_____
_____
_____

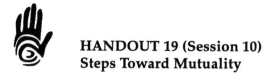

HANDOUT 19 (Session 10)
Steps Toward Mutuality

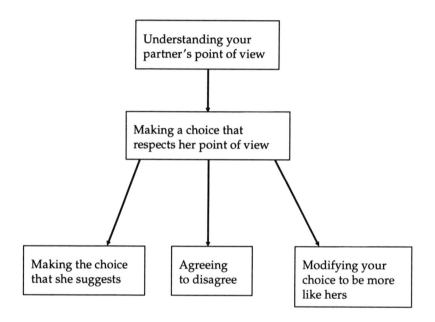

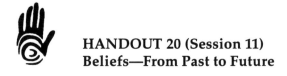

HANDOUT 20 (Session 11)
Beliefs—From Past to Future

Examination of beliefs that underlie your actions toward your partner and influence your relationship has been a focus of this group.

At this point, it is useful to reflect on how your actions and beliefs have changed.

Think about your old beliefs, your new beliefs, and your new behaviors in relation to the topics covered in this program.

Area	Old Belief	New Belief	New Behavior
Definition of abuse	_____	_____	_____
	_____	_____	_____
Choosing to be abusive	_____	_____	_____
Self-monitoring	_____	_____	_____
	_____	_____	_____
Feelings	_____	_____	_____
	_____	_____	_____
Relationships	_____	_____	_____
	_____	_____	_____
Consequences of abuse	_____	_____	_____
Connecting through listening	_____	_____	_____
Equality and disagreement	_____	_____	_____
Mutuality in relationships	_____	_____	_____

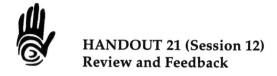 **HANDOUT 21 (Session 12)**
Review and Feedback

At the conclusion of this group process, it is useful to take stock of what has happened and what still needs to occur for you.

It is useful to have your own thoughts about this as well as the observations of the other group members.

Therefore, as a closing exercise, each group member in turn is asked to respond to the following questions:

About myself:

1. What is the most important change that I have made as a result of this group?
2. What do I still have to change?

About each group member (in turn):

3. What was a positive change that I observed in this person?
4. What do I see in this person that still needs more work?

About each group leader:

5. What did he or she do that was particularly helpful?
6. What do I wish he or she would have done?

References

Adams, D. (1989). Feminist-based interventions for battering men. In P. L. Caesar & L. K. Hamberger (Eds.), *Treating men who batter: Theory, practice, and programs* (pp. 3-23). New York: Springer.

Almeida, R. V., & Bograd, M. (1991). Sponsorship: Holding men accountable for domestic violence. *Journal of Feminist Family Therapy, 2*, 243-259.

Ball-Rokeach, S. J., Rokeach, M., & Grube, J. W. (1984). *The great American values test: Influencing behavior and belief through television.* New York: Free Press.

Beutler, L. E., & Bergan, J. (1991). Value change in counseling and psychotherapy. *Journal of Counseling Psychology, 38*, 16-24.

Caesar, P. L. (1985, August). *The wife-beater: Personality and psychosocial characteristics.* Paper presented at the annual meeting of the American Psychological Association, Los Angeles.

Campbell, A. (1991). *Men, women and aggression.* New York: Basic Books.

Chodorow, N. (1978). *The reproduction of mothering.* Berkeley: University of California Press.

DeBono, K. G., & Harnish, R. J. (1988). Source expertise, source attractiveness, and the processing of persuasive information: A functional approach. *Journal of Personality and Social Psychology, 55*, 541-546.

Doyle, J. A. (1983). *The male experience.* Dubuque, IA: William C. Brown.

Dutton, D. G. (1988). *The domestic assault of women: Psychological and criminal justice perspectives.* Boston: Allyn & Bacon.

Dutton, D. G., & Strachan, C. E. (1987, July). *The prediction of recidivism in a population of wife assaulters.* Paper presented at the Third National Conference on Family Violence, Durham, NH.

166

Edleson, J. F., & Tolman, R. M. (1992). *Intervention for men who batter.* Newbury Park, CA: Sage.

Feazell, C. S., Mayers, R. S., & Deschner, J. (1984). Services for men who batter: Implications for programs and policies. *Family Relations, 33,* 217-223.

Gilligan, C. (1982). *In a different voice: Psychological theory and women's development.* Cambridge, MA: Harvard University Press.

Glaser, B., & Kirschenbaum, H. (1980). Using values clarification in counseling settings. *Personnel and Guidance Journal, 58,* 569-575.

Gondolf, E. W. (1985). Anger and oppression in men who batter: Empiricist and feminist perspectives and their implications for research. *Victimology: An International Journal, 10,* 311-324.

Gondolf, E. W. (1986). Evaluating programs for men who batter: Problems and perspectives. *Journal of Family Violence, 2,* 95-108.

Grusznski, R. J., & Carrillo, T. P. (1988). Who completes batterers' treatment groups? An empirical investigation. *Journal of Family Violence, 3,* 141-150.

Hart, B. (1988). *Safety for women: Monitoring batterer's programs.* Harrisburg: Pennsylvania Coalition Against Domestic Violence.

Hoffman, M. (1977). Sex differences in empathy and related behaviors. *Psychological Bulletin, 84,* 712-722.

Hotaling, G. T., & Sugarman, D. B. (1986). Analysis of risk markers in husband to wife violence. *Violence and Victims, 1,* 101-124.

Hotaling, G. T., & Sugarman, D. B. (1990). Prevention of wife assault. In R. T. Ammerman & M. Hersen (Eds.), *Treatment of family violence: A sourcebook* (pp. 385-405). New York: John Wiley.

Hudson, W. W. (1982). *The clinical measurement package: A field manual.* Homewood, IL: Dorsey.

Jenkins, A. (1990). *Invitation to responsibility: The therapeutic engagement of men who are violent and abusive.* Adelaide, South Australia: Dulwich Centre.

Jordan, J. V. (1991). Empathy and self boundaries. In J. V. Jordan, A. G. Kaplan, J. B. Miller, I. P. Striver, & J. L. Surrey (Eds.), *Women's growth in connection: Writings from the Stone Center* (pp. 67-80). New York: Guilford.

Jordan, J. V., Kaplan, A. G., Miller, J. B., Striver, I. P., & Surrey, J. L. (Eds.). (1991). *Women's growth in connection: Writings from the Stone Center.* New York: Guilford.

Kahle, L. R. (1983). *Social values and social change: Adaptation to live in America.* New York: Praeger.

Kahle, L. R. (1984). *Attitudes and social adaptation: A person-situation interaction.* New York: Pergamon.

Klugel, J. R., & Smith, E. R. (1986). *Beliefs about inequality: American views of what is and what ought to be.* New York: Aldine.

Kuypers, J. A. (1992). *Man's will to hurt: Investigating the causes and supports and varieties of his violence.* Halifax, Nova Scotia: Fernwood.

Langer, E. J. (1989). Minding matters: The consequences of mindlessness-mindfulness. *Advances in Experimental Social Psychology, 22,* 137-168.

London, P. (1964). *The models and morals of psychotherapy.* New York: Holt, Rinehart & Winston.

Maiuro, R. D., Cahn, T. S., & Vitaliano, P. P. (1986). Assertiveness deficits and hostility in domestically violent men. *Violence and Victims, 1,* 279-289.

Miller, J. B. (1986). *What do we mean by relationships?* (Work in Progress No. 22). Wellesley, MA: Stone Center.

Miller, J. B. (1991). The development of women's sense of self. In J. V. Jordan, A. G. Kaplan, J. B. Miller, I. P. Stiver, & J. L. Surrey (Eds.), *Women's growth in connection: Writings from the Stone Center* (pp. 11-26). New York: Guilford.

Moore, D., & Haverkamp, B. E. (1989). Measured increases in male emotional expressiveness following a structured group intervention. *Journal of Counselling and Development, 67*, 513-517.

Murphy, C. M., & Cascardi, M. (1993). Psychological aggression and abuse in marriage. In R. L. Hampton, T. P. Gullotta, G. R. Adams, E. H. Potter III, & R. P. Weissberg (Eds.), *Family violence: Prevention and treatment* (pp. 86-112). Newbury Park, CA: Sage.

Neidig, P. H., Friedman, D. H., & Collins, B. S. (1984, July). *Attitudinal characteristics of men who have engaged in spousal abuse.* Paper presented at the Second National Conference for Family Violence Research, Durham, NH.

Nicholas, M. (1984). *Change in the context of group therapy.* New York: Brunner/Mazel.

Pasick, R. (1990). Raised to work. In R. L. Meth & R. S. Pasick (Eds.), *Men in therapy: The challenge of change* (pp. 35-53). New York: Guilford.

Pasick, R. S., Gordon, S., & Meth, R. L. (1990). Helping men understand themselves. In R. L. Meth & R. S. Pasick (Eds.), *Men in therapy: The challenge of change* (pp. 152-180). New York: Guilford.

Pence, E., & Paymar, M. (1993). *Education groups for men who batter: The Duluth model.* New York: Springer.

Petty, R. E., & Cacioppo, J. T. (1986). *Communication and persuasion: Central and peripheral routes to attitude change.* New York: Springer-Verlag.

Pirog-Good, M., & Stets-Kealy, J. (1985, Summer). Male batterers and battering prevention programs: A national survey. *Response*, pp. 8-12.

Pleck, J. H. (1983). *The myth of masculinity.* Cambridge: MIT Press.

Ptacek, J. (1988). Why do men batter their wives? In K. Yllö & M. Bograd (Eds.), *Feminist perspectives on wife abuse* (pp. 133-157). Newbury Park, CA: Sage.

Raths, L. E., Harmin, M., & Simon, S. B. (1966). *Values and teaching: Working with values in the classroom.* Columbus, OH: Merrill.

Rich, A. (1979). *On lies, secrets, and silence: Selected prose 1966-1979.* New York: Norton.

Roberts, A. R. (1984). *Battered women and their families: Intervention strategies and treatment programs.* New York: Springer.

Rokeach, M. (1967). *Value survey.* Palo Alto, CA: Consulting Psychologists Press.

Rokeach, M. (1973). *The nature of human values.* New York: Free Press.

Rokeach, M. (1979). *Understanding human values: Individual and societal.* New York: Free Press.

Rokeach, M. (1985). Inducing change and stability in belief systems and personality structures. *Journal of Social Issues, 41*, 153-171.

Rokeach, M., & Regan, J. F. (1980). The role of values in counseling situations. *Personnel and Guidance Journal, 58*, 576-583.

Rose, S. D. (1989). *Working with adults in groups.* San Francisco: Jossey-Bass.

Rosenbaum, A. (1986). Of men, macho and marital violence. *Journal of Family Violence, 1*, 121-130.

Rosenbaum, A., & O'Leary, K. D. (1981). Marital violence: Characteristics of abusive couples. *Journal of Consulting and Clinical Psychology, 49*, 63-71.

Rosenthal, D. (1955). Changes in some moral values following psychotherapy. *Journal of Consulting Psychology, 6*, 431-436.

Saunders, D. G. (1989). Cognitive and behavioral interventions with men who batter: Application and outcome. In P. L. Caesar & L. K. Hamberger (Eds.), *Treating men who batter: Theory, practice, and programs* (pp. 77-100). New York: Springer.

Saunders, D. G. (1992). Woman battering. In R. T. Ammerman & M. Hersen (Eds.), *Assessment of family violence: A clinical and legal sourcebook* (pp. 208-235). New York: John Wiley.

Sigler, R. T. (1989). *Domestic violence in context: An assessment of community attitudes.* Lexington, MA: Lexington Books.

Straus, M. A. (1979). Measuring intrafamily violence and conflict: The Conflict Tactics Scale. *Journal of Marriage and the Family, 41,* 75-88.

Strauss, A., & Corbin, J. (1990). *Basics of qualitative research: Grounded theory procedures and techniques.* Newbury Park, CA: Sage.

Stockton, R., & Moran, D. K. (1982). Review and perspectives of critical dimensions in therapeutic small group research. In G. M. Gazda (Ed.), *Basic approaches to group psychotherapy* (3rd ed., pp. 37-85). Springfield, IL: Charles C Thomas.

Surrey, J. L. (1991). The "self-in relation": A theory of women's development. In J. V. Jordan, A. G. Kaplan, J. B. Miller, I. P. Striver, & J. L. Surrey (Eds.), *Women's growth in connection: Writings from the Stone Center* (pp. 51-66). New York: Guilford.

Telch, C. F., & Lindquist, C. V. (1984). Violent versus non-violent couples: A comparison of patterns. *Psychotherapy, 21,* 242-248.

Thompson, L., & Walker, A. J. (1989). Gender in families: Women and men in marriage, work and parenthood. *Journal of Marriage and the Family, 51,* 845-871.

Tolman, R. M. (1989). The development of a measure of psychological maltreatment of women by their male partners. *Violence and Victims, 4,* 159-177.

Tolman, R. M. (1990). *The impact of group process and outcome of groups for men who batter.* Paper presented at the European Congress on the Advancement of Behavior Therapy, Paris.

Tolman, R. M., & Bennett, L. W. (1990). A review of quantitative research on men who batter. *Journal of Interpersonal Violence, 5,* 87-118.

Tolman, R. M., & Bhosley, G. (1991). The outcome of participation in a shelter-sponsored program for men who batter. In D. D. Knudsen & J. L. Miller (Eds.), *Abused and battered: Social and legal responses to family violence* (pp. 113-122). New York: Aldine.

Weiss, R. S. (1990). *Staying the course: The emotional lives of men who do well at work.* New York: Free Press.

Williams, D. G. (1988). Gender, marriage and psychosocial well-being. *Journal of Family Issues, 9,* 452-468.

Williams, R. M. (1979). Change and stability in values and value systems. A sociological perspective. In M. Rokeach (Ed.), *Understanding human values: Individual and societal* (pp. 15-46). New York: Free Press.

Wood, J. T. (1993). Engendered relations: Interaction, caring, power, and responsibility in intimacy. In S. Duck (Ed.), *Social context and relationships* (pp. 26-54). Newbury Park, CA: Sage.

Yalom, I. (1975). *The theory and practice of group psychotherapy.* New York: Basic Books.

Yllö, K. (1984). Sexual equality and violence against wives in American states. *Journal of Comparative Family Studies, 1,* 67-86.

Index

About the Author

Mary Nõmme Russell is Associate Professor in the School of Social Work, University of British Columbia. She has published numerous articles and several books on topics that include wife abuse, social work research, and feminist counseling. She has co-led groups for wife abusers for several years at Family Services of Greater Vancouver as well as conducted research on their family violence program. She is on the board of the B.C. Institute on Family Violence, as well as the editorial board of the *Canadian Social Work Review*. She completed her M.S.W. at the University of British Columbia and her Ph.D. in clinical psychology at Simon Fraser University.